Levels and Transitions
in Children's Development

Kurt W. Fischer, *Editor*

NEW DIRECTIONS FOR CHILD DEVELOPMENT
WILLIAM DAMON, *Editor-in-Chief*

Number 21, September 1983

Paperback sourcebooks in
The Jossey-Bass Social and Behavioral Sciences Series

Jossey-Bass Inc., Publishers
San Francisco • Washington • London

Kurt W. Fischer (Ed.).
Levels and Transitions in Children's Development.
New Directions for Child Development, no. 21.
San Francisco: Jossey-Bass, 1983.

New Directions for Child Development Series
William Damon, *Editor-in-Chief*

New Directions for Child Development (publication number
USPS 494-090) is published quarterly by Jossey-Bass Inc., Publishers.
Second-class postage rates are paid at San Francisco, California,
and at additional mailing offices.

Correspondence:
Subscriptions, single-issue orders, change of address notices,
undelivered copies, and other correspondence should be sent to
New Directions Subscriptions, Jossey-Bass Inc., Publishers,
433 California Street, San Francisco, California 94104.

Editorial correspondence should be sent to the Editor-in-Chief,
William Damon, Department of Psychology, Clark University,
Worcester, Massachusetts 01610.

Library of Congress Catalogue Card Number LC 83-82343
International Standard Serial Number ISSN 0195-2269
International Standard Book Number ISBN 87589-933-1

Cover art by Willi Baum
Manufactured in the United States of America

Ordering Information

The paperback sourcebooks listed below are published quarterly and can be ordered either by subscription or single-copy.

Subscriptions cost $35.00 per year for institutions, agencies, and libraries. Individuals can subscribe at the special rate of $21.00 per year *if payment is by personal check.* (Note that the full rate of $35.00 applies if payment is by institutional check, even if the subscription is designated for an individual.) Standing orders are accepted. Subscriptions normally begin with the first of the four sourcebooks in the current publication year of the series. When ordering, please indicate if you prefer your subscription to begin with the first issue of the *coming* year.

Single copies are available at $7.95 when payment accompanies order, and *all single-copy orders under $25.00 must include payment.* (California, New Jersey, New York, and Washington, D.C., residents please include appropriate sales tax.) For billed orders, cost per copy is $7.95 plus postage and handling. (Prices subject to change without notice.)

Bulk orders (ten or more copies) of any individual sourcebook are available at the following discounted prices: 10–49 copies, $7.15 each; 50–100 copies, $6.35 each; over 100 copies, *inquire.* Sales tax and postage and handling charges apply as for single copy orders.

To ensure correct and prompt delivery, all orders must give either the *name of an individual* or an *official purchase order number.* Please submit your order as follows:

Subscriptions: specify series and year subscription is to begin.
Single Copies: specify sourcebook code (such as, CD8) and first two words of title.

Mail orders for United States and Possessions, Latin America, Canada, Japan, Australia, and New Zealand to:
 Jossey-Bass Inc., Publishers
 433 California Street
 San Francisco, California 94104

Mail orders for all other parts of the world to:
 Jossey-Bass Limited
 28 Banner Street
 London EC1Y 8QE

New Directions for Child Development Series
William Damon, *Editor-in-Chief*

CD1 *Social Cognition,* William Damon
CD2 *Moral Development,* William Damon
CD3 *Early Symbolization,* Howard Gardner, Dennie Wolf
CD4 *Social Interaction and Communication During Infancy,* Ina C. Uzgiris
CD5 *Intellectual Development Beyond Childhood,* Deanna Kuhn
CD6 *Fact, Fiction, and Fantasy in Childhood,* Ellen Winner, Howard Gardner

Contents

Editor's Notes: The Search for Developmental Levels

Traditionally, stages have played a central role in the study of development. Indeed, the main tool for portraying psychological development of any sort has been the description of a series of stages of behavioral change. In recent years, however, the stage hypothesis has fallen into disrepute because of the consistent failure of research to support stage theories. Fortunately, a number of investigators have been searching for alternative descriptions of development, and the main purpose of this sourcebook is to present some particularly promising research based on those new formulations.

The most commonly accepted empirical criterion for the occurrence of a stage has been developmental *synchrony*: That is, when children enter a new stage, most or all of their behaviors are supposed to shift to that stage within a short time. According to Piaget (1957), for example, the child's mind in general should move from concrete operations to formal operations at 10-to-12 years of age. But research that has focused on verifying such synchrony has consistently failed to find it (Fischer and Bullock, 1981; Flavell, 1971). As a result, many developmentalists have fallen back on a lesser meaning for stage: They use stages as nothing more than descriptive tools for portraying developmental change in terms of a series of arbitrary, sequential dividing points.

The authors of this sourcebook all have good reason to argue for a richer definition of stage. Using empirical criteria other than synchrony, they have found evidence for major reorganizations in psychological development. In general, the authors do avoid the problematic term *stage* and substitute other terms such as *level* or *transition*. A developmental *level* refers to a general reorganization or qualitative change in children's behavior and can occur even when the synchrony criterion is not met for a particular level. A *transition* occurs when a child moves from one level of organization to another. In Chapter One, Kurt Fischer provides a conceptual framework for the sourcebook. He suggests a new empirical criterion for the existence of a developmental level: a discontinuity in the form of the developmental function for some behavior or characteristic — that is, a sudden change in the pattern of growth of a behavior. This criterion appears to fit the evidence for levels reported in all

Preparation of this entire volume was supported by a grant from the Carnegie Corporation of New York. The statements made and views expressed are solely the responsibility of the authors. I would like to thank Marilyn Pelot for her help with the volume.

1

the other chapters. In general, eight developmental levels seem to occur in sequence during the first sixteen years of life.

The rest of the chapters present the evidence and arguments for levels in roughly the chronological order in which these levels develop. Michelle Lampl and Robert Emde (Chapter Two) outline some of the evidence for the first two levels in early infancy and present new data on the episodic or discontinuous nature of physical growth during this period. Philip Zelazo and Elizabeth Leonard (Chapter Three) focus on the third developmental level in infancy—the period when a child becomes able to generate ideas about an object or event. In Chapter Four, Roberta Corrigan also presents evidence for the existence of the third level, but her major focus is on the cluster of developmental changes marking the fourth level, where mental representational skills emerge at about two years of age. Robert McCall (Chapter Five) describes his own project, in which he used a novel method to locate the transitions in the performance on infant intelligence tests during infancy. His findings demonstrate the same four levels outlined by the previous authors.

Although much of the research on developmental levels has focused on infancy, a few investigators have searched systematically for evidence of such levels in the childhood years. A number of their findings clearly support the existence of discontinuities at certain age periods. In Chapter Six, Sheryl Kenny outlines those findings and provides a general characterization of the four levels that seem to emerge between two and sixteen years of age.

In general, one of the important differences between the developmental-levels framework and traditional stage approaches is that levels are hypothesized to result from a particular combination of organismic and environmental factors. Levels cannot be construed simply as a characteristic of the child, since children routinely seem to demonstrate a range of different levels in different environments. The concept of stage has always tended to lead toward nativist interpretations, as if stages merely unfolded under genetic control, without substantive environmental contributions. Several of the authors (Fischer, McCall, Kenny, and Bullock) address this issue directly, arguing that environmental contributions are fundamental to developmental levels and transitions. In Chapter Seven, Daniel Bullock carries this argument the furthest, arguing that social relationships play an integral role in cognitive transitions. Indeed, social support commonly causes children to perform beyond the "highest" capabilities that they can demonstrate when acting alone. Bullock suggests that cognitive activity and social behavior are fundamentally intertwined in human intelligence.

This sourcebook seeks to bring together a number of different but closely related projects that all converge on a similar set of conclusions: Children progress through a series of levels that are evidenced by discontinuities or sudden changes in the development of behaviors; there is substantial although not complete agreement on the nature and timing of these levels. To explain the evidence for the levels, new theoretical frameworks are needed that incorporate the interaction between the child and his or her environment as the basis for explaining developmental change.

Kurt W. Fischer
Editor

References

Fischer, K. W., and Bullock, D. "Patterns of Data: Sequence, Synchrony, and Constraint in Cognitive Development." In K. W. Fischer (Ed.), *Cognitive Development.* New Directions for Child Development, no. 12. San Francisco: Jossey-Bass, 1981.

Flavell, J. H. "Stage-Related Properties of Cognitive Development." *Cognitive Psychology,* 1971, *2,* 421–453.

Piaget, J. "Logique et équilibre dans les Comportements du Sujet." *Études d'Épistémologie Génétique,* 1957, *2,* 27–118.

Kurt W. Fischer is associate professor of psychology at the University of Denver and director of the Cognitive Development Laboratory. His interests include the nature of developmental change and the relations among social, cognitive, emotional, and physical development.

Developmental levels appear to be marked by discontinuities — that is, sudden spurts or changes in behavior. Both characteristics of the child and environmental conditions determine when and how these discontinuities occur.

Developmental Levels as Periods of Discontinuity

Kurt W. Fischer

Suppose that a team of developmental researchers stumbled upon a genuine stage in the development of some behavior. Would they be able to detect the stage that was right there in front of them? If they did notice it, how would they know what they had found? How would they be able to tell that it was a stage? What pattern of results would they look for? Despite the hundreds of studies of psychological development in recent decades, these questions still have no definitive answers. There is no uniform empirical criterion used by developmental researchers to determine when they have found a stage. The traditional stage theories have failed to provide consistent definitions of *stage* that can be practically applied in research, and therefore it has not been possible to reach any consensus about whether stages really exist — or even what they are (Broughton, 1981; Fischer and Bullock, 1981; Flavell, 1983).

While the traditional definitions of stage have failed, new research and theory promise to substantially simplify and clarify the portrait of the nature of stages in development. Behaviors do show systematic change — that is,

Preparation of this chapter was supported by a grant from the Carnegie Corporation of New York. The statements made and views expressed are solely the responsibility of the author. I would like to thank the following individuals for their help on various parts of this chapter: Daniel Bullock, Richard Canfield, Susan Harter, Marilyn Pelot, Sandra Pipp, and Lori Walter.

K. W. Fischer (Ed.). *Levels and Transitions in Children's Development.* New Directions for Child Development, no. 21. San Francisco: Jossey-Bass, September 1983.

development—which can be described precisely in terms of developmental sequences. At certain points in development, these sequences seem to show discontinuities, or sharp alterations in the form of the curve portraying developmental change. The nature and timing of the alterations can be strongly affected by many environmental conditions, but these effects appear to be systematic and predictable. Starting with this discontinuity criterion, an examination of the research literature yields evidence of a number of major developmental discontinuities. These will be termed *levels* because they do not share some of the characteristics usually associated with the definition of stage.

The Criteria for Levels

The most common definition of stage, which comes from the Piagetian tradition, has involved a list of approximately half a dozen abstract characteristics. To show stages, a developmental sequence must, at a minimum (1) show qualitative change, (2) include later developmental steps that are hierarchically built upon previous ones, (3) lead to a structure of the whole (*structure d'ensemble*), a Gestalt-like logical structure, (4) reflect an equilibrium, (5) show movement toward an end point, and (6) be universal across children and cultures (Kohlberg, 1969; Piaget, 1957). The patterns of developmental change required by such a list of criteria have never been adequately explained, but at least two criteria have been maintained consistently in the literature: (1) All children must pass through the same fixed sequence of developmental steps within each behavioral domain. (2) There should be high synchrony across domains for some steps in the sequence as the child establishes a new equilibrium, that is, reaches the next stage (Fischer and Bullock, 1981).

Neither of these criteria has withstood empirical test (Biggs and Collis, 1982; Feldman, 1980; Fischer, 1980; Flavell, 1983). High synchrony between behaviors at one stage has proved difficult to find even for two potentially related domains—for example, two types of perspective-taking tasks that are both designed to measure the development of concrete operations (Rubin, 1973). The fixed nature of developmental sequences also has not been supported either across cultures or across children within a culture. Consequently, researchers have begun to abandon the concept of stage and have fallen back on less stringent descriptive concepts, such as *level*. The most common criterion for determining whether a level exists is simply qualitative change in a behavior.

A substantial problem still arises from the use of this criterion, however. Developmentally ordered qualitative changes occur every time a child learns anything new. When a 5-year-old girl succeeds in tying her shoe for the first time, she shows a qualitative change in behavior; yet this change by itself should not count as evidence of a major reorganization. It is merely one step in a developmental sequence composed of many steps, not a genuine level. Although it may make sense, for descriptive purposes, to say that any qualitative change denoting a consistent developmental ordering shows a level, most existing cognitive-developmental theories predict that there are periods of major behavioral reorganization that really do deserve to be called levels. The question is, how can these levels be detected in research? For the team of developmental researchers who have happened upon a level, how will they know they have found it? How can they determine if the behavior they see reflects merely another everyday qualitative change or something grander?

Discontinuities and Continuities

One promising criterion for levels has been generally neglected by investigators until recently. A *discontinuity* occurs whenever there is a rapid or sharp change in the form of a developmental curve. For example, the sharp rise in the dotted line in Figure 1 depicts one type of discontinuous change, while the gradual rise in the solid line shows a continuous change. The meaning of discontinuity will be restricted here to a rapid change in the form of a developmental function, because other meanings are not relevant to the present argument (Wohlwill, 1973). In any case, developmental theorists commonly have assumed that entrance to a new stage produces a relatively sudden transformation in a child's behavior (Werner, 1957).

Several investigators have suggested recently that spurts or other types of discontinuities might serve as criteria for developmental levels. Case (1980) states that "learning explosions" may occur at a few points in development where dramatic reorganizations occur. White and Emde and others (1976) argue that shifts in biobehavioral capacities mark new developmental levels. Epstein (1978) hypothesizes that spurts in brain growth may correlate closely with Piagetian stages. Fischer and Pipp (forthcoming) postulate that spurts occur for each of a series of at least ten developmental levels, which unfold between birth and 30 years of age. Hand (1981) and McCall (1979 and this volume) argue that more complex types of discontinuities may reflect major reorganizations across a series of developmental levels.

Detecting Discontinuities. Most studies are not designed to detect discontinuities, perhaps because investigators have not recognized their relevance to the issue of levels. However, designs and measures that can test for discontinuities are relatively straightforward and can be readily incorporated into ongoing research. Fischer and others (forthcoming) provide an overview of the logic and methods needed to detect discontinuities.

In most developmental studies, the type of discontinuity that is simplest to identify is the spurt, in which performance shows a large and rapid increase as illustrated in Figure 1. To detect such a discontinuity, the investigator needs both a "ruler" to measure the size of the developmental change and a "clock" to measure its speed. Guttman-type scales, in which a series of tasks

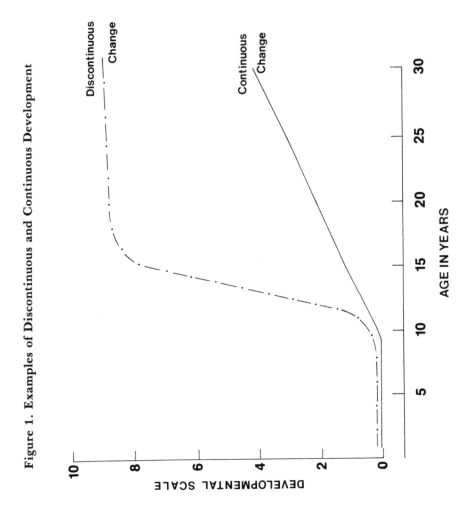

Figure 1. Examples of Discontinuous and Continuous Development

forms a developmental sequence, are particularly useful in measuring how large a change is, but any relatively continuous scale can be used. Age is the most common scale for speed of change, but any other index of rate of development can be used. Indeed, methods are available that can detect discontinuities even when different children undergo change at widely varying ages.

Environmental Conditions. In addition to developing the proper measures for change, the researcher must also ask another question: Under which environmental conditions will development be discontinuous, and under which ones will it be continuous? The research evidence to date indicates that the form of the developmental function will vary greatly under differing conditions.

Most developmental studies that include an assessment of a developmental function seem to show continuous change like the solid curve in Figure 1 — that is, slow, gradual improvement with age. For example, Colby and others (1983) used the Moral Judgment Interview to investigate the development of Kohlberg's moral stages during a period of more than twenty years. Although the investigators argue that their longitudinal data support a stage model, which implies periods of discontinuous change, the form of the developmental function for each stage was very similar to the solid curve in Figure 1. For example, use of Stage 4 reasoning first appeared in subjects' responses at 13 years of age and increased very slowly over the entire 20 years of the study. Not until 32 to 33 years of age did subjects respond with stage 4 reasoning over 50 percent of the time (Fischer, 1983).

There are some studies that show spurts or other discontinuities in the developmental function, including those reported by the authors in this sourcebook, but they constitute a relatively small proportion of the studies that could have found discontinuities. What accounts for the differences in the research findings?

One possibility is that some set of environmental or testing conditions produces discontinuous functions, while another set produces continuous functions. In most of the studies that have found continuous functions, the conditions seem to have been as follows: Subjects were tested only once on relatively unfamiliar tasks, and they were not given any opportunity to practice the tasks nor any model of good answers. They were brought into a testing room and asked to perform the tasks, often with some time limit; then they left the room and were never seen by the researchers again. Studies that have produced discontinuous functions, on the other hand, seem typically to have involved a different set of conditions. The subject was tested on highly familiar materials, allowed to practice the tasks, or shown good answers to use as models. These conditions give an individual an opportunity to work with the tasks long enough to perform well. Thus, studies designed to elicit optimal performance seem to be more likely to uncover developmental discontinuities.

Also, a disproportionate number of studies reporting discontinuities appear to involve infants. In this sourcebook, four of the five chapters that describe research projects on discontinuities concern subjects 2 years of age or younger. Although it may be just coincidental that most research has been conducted on discontinuities in infancy, several scholars have suggested that infants are naturally motivated to perform at or near their optimal capacity (Hand, 1981; Wallon, 1970). This motivational pattern apparently changes during the preschool years, when children appear to begin performing below their optimum on a regular basis. If infants routinely function at or near their optimal capacity, they would spontaneously show discontinuities more frequently than older children.

An Upper Limit on Performance

A reasonable interpretation of findings to date, then, is that under conditions that produce optimal performance, discontinuous development will be the rule. Under conditions that make optimal performance unlikely, continuous development will normally occur. One formulation that predicts exactly this pattern of findings is the optimal-level hypothesis, based on skill theory (Fischer and Bullock, 1981; Fischer and Pipp, forthcoming): When children move to a new cognitive-developmental level, they show an increase in their highest capacity—the upper limit on the complexity of skills that they can control. A child's optimal performance will suddenly increase, or show a spurt, when he or she enters a new developmental level. Most of a person's everyday behavior, however, does not reflect this upper limit and so will demonstrate continuous rather than discontinuous change.

Besides skill theory, several other neo-Piagetian approaches incorporate hypotheses of an upper limit on performance, although the exact form of the limit differs from theory to theory. For example, Biggs and Collis (1982) hypothesize that most behavior in the classroom does not reflect children's best capabilities. One of a teacher's primary tasks should be to help children move toward their upper limit for classroom activities. Case (1980) and Halford (1982) suggest that there is an upper limit to the number of items that children can hold in working memory. Consequently, they cannot learn any tasks requiring a larger number of items in memory, but they can master tasks that entail a smaller memory load. In some of these theories, the upper-limit concept does not appear to be linked to developmental spurts. A continuous, monotonic increase in the upper limit for behavior is described, with no periods of discontinuity in the rate of increase. According to this continuity hypothesis, there is a genuine upper bound on the type of scheme or skill children can construct, but that upper bound increases gradually and smoothly throughout childhood. The upper bound for such behaviors thus does not delineate any clearcut developmental levels.

Skill theory, on the other hand, posits that the upper limit on performance is directly tied to developmental discontinuities (Fischer, 1980). When children enter a new cognitive level, their optimal performance will show spurts in virtually all domains where they perform at or near their upper limit. The result will be a cluster of spurts within the age region where a new level emerges. (Of course, individuals do not perform optimally in many domains and will therefore show no behavioral spurts in those areas.)

Consider an adolescent girl who is entering the level termed single abstractions, which typically emerges at 10 to 13 years of age in middle-class children. At 10 years, she shows the very first spurt to this level of thinking in one domain—the way she thinks about the kind of person she is (honest, sincere, and so forth) when she is with her best friend. Then, at various times during the period between 10 and 13 years, her optimal performance will spurt in a broad array of other domains, producing a cluster of discontinuities in performance. Note that the discontinuities are neither perfectly synchronous nor instantaneous. They merely occur relatively quickly and within a limited age interval.

In general, the pattern of data that indicates the emergence of a new developmental level is a cluster of spurts in optimal performance in a range of domains. For the individual child, the cluster is usually restricted to a specific age period, but across children there may be substantial variation in the ages at which the cluster of spurts occurs. Also, although a discontinuity in any single domain can suggest the emergence of a new developmental level, it cannot provide definitive evidence because the spurt might result from something specific to that domain. For example, a 9-year-old boy might attain a new, more general understanding of how to add, and his performance at addition will spurt as a result, although he is not necessarily entering a new level. A cluster of spurts across domains will not result from any such specific effect, however, and will provide a powerful index of a new developmental level (Fischer and Bullock, 1981).

A Series of Developmental Levels

Whether or not the optimal-level hypothesis proves to be correct, the search for discontinuities has uncovered many interesting findings, with a surprising degree of consensus among researchers. Taken together, the studies discussed in this sourcebook support the existence of at least eight developmental levels (see Table 1). Each level is marked by a period of discontinuities in various developmental functions, including cognition, play, social behavior, language, and physical development. The descriptions of the levels here are based primarily on the analyses by the authors in this sourcebook.

First Sensorimotor Level. The first developmental level, appearing at 2 to 4 months of age, involves the emergence of sensorimotor intelligence and the first clear social-emotional responsiveness to a caregiver. During this transition, infants move from the newborn period, in which their behavior is basically reflexive, to the first level of sensorimotor development, in which their

Table 1. Eight Developmental Levels Supported by Evidence of Discontinuities

Level	Characteristics	Relevant Chapters	Modal Age of Emergence
First Sensorimotor Level	Single actions and perceptions; first social-emotional responsiveness.	Emde and Lampl McCall	2 to 4 months
Second Sensorimotor Level	Separation of means from ends in action; establishment of attachment relationship.	Emde and Lampl McCall	7 to 8 months
Third Sensorimotor Level	Location of characteristics in objects and people; sensorimotor "hypotheses"; use of single words.	Corrigan McCall Zelazo and Leonard	11 to 13 months
Representations	Symbolization of people and objects; use of short sentences.	Bullock Corrigan McCall	18 to 24 months
Simple Relations of Representations	Coordination of two or more categories; simplified concrete operations tasks.	Kenny	4 to 5 years
Concrete Operations	Coordination of multiple, complex categories; traditional concrete operations tasks.	Kenny	6 to 8 years
Beginning Formal Operations	Abstractions; hypothetical ideas; simple formal operations tasks.	Kenny	10 to 12 years
Later Formal Operations	Coordination of abstractions; most of traditional formal operations tasks.	Kenny	14 to 16 years

behavior is organized around single actions and perceptions without any differentiation of self from the outside world. For example, babies at this level first exhibit the social smile in response to another person's face, visually follow a ball that moves in front of their faces, and move their hand to grasp a toy that grazes the edge of their hand. They also begin to sleep through the night and to show more stable brainwave patterns.

Second Sensorimotor Level. The next level emerges at 7 to 8 months when babies begin separating means from ends in sensorimotor actions and establishing attachment relationships with their caregivers. Infants start to use one action to bring about another, as when they remove an obstacle to grasp a toy hidden under it. They begin imitating competently the actions and vocalizations of others, and vocalization becomes important in their own behavior too, especially in social interactions. At this level, babies also start showing unambiguous separation distress (when separated from their mothers) and stranger distress (when a stranger approaches).

Third Sensorimotor Level. A more sophisticated form of sensorimotor intelligence emerges at 11 to 13 months when babies begin to understand that objects, people, and events have certain constant properties. They also start to use single words in speech and establish a more stable relationship with their caregivers. In general, babies at this age seem to bring coherent sets of expectations—sensorimotor "hypotheses"—to bear upon their experiences with things in the world. For example, an infant handles a new object by trying out various actions on it.

Representation. Infants move beyond sensorimotor intelligence to a strong form of representation at 18 to 24 months. The spurts most obvious to parents and other caregivers involve language: Children learn a large number of new words and begin to form many two- and three-word utterances (sentences). The symbolic activity of pretend play and a wide range of cognitive and social skills seem to surge forward, including the abilities to flexibly seriate nesting cups and to understand that another person can surreptitiously hide an object.

These four levels of infant development have been supported by a wide range of research besides that included in this sourcebook. (For a review, see Fischer, 1982.) Uzgiris (1976) was one of the first to systematically describe the four levels, based on her longitudinal study of infant development. A recent study by Seibert and others (in press) even found that retarded, handicapped children showed the same four levels in development. The children were tested on the Bayley infant scale, the Uzgiris-Hunt sensorimotor scales, and a new test called the Early Social-Communication Scales. The shift to each of the first three levels for retarded children occurred at the mental age (based on the Bayley infant scale) that corresponded with the chronological age of the shift in normal infants. The correspondence was less clearcut for the fourth level.

Simple Relations of Representations. The ability to combine representations in simple relations seems to develop at approximately 4 to 5 years of
age. Children begin relating one social category to another, such as *doctor* to
patient. In simple concrete situations, they relate their own perspective to that
of another person and thus understand that the two are different. Children can
even carry out simplified forms of many of Piaget's concrete operations tasks,
such as transitivity and conservation. A number of neo-Piagetian theorists
have hypothesized a separate developmental level during this age period (Biggs
and Collis, 1982; Case, 1980; Fischer, 1980; Halford, 1982; Siegler, 1981),
although Piaget (1970) did not designate any major reorganization at this
time. Of all the levels portrayed in this sourcebook, this one has been investigated the least. Nevertheless, there are not only a number of theories suggesting changes during this period but also various studies documenting developmental discontinuities, such as spurts in counting skills and language abilities
(Fuson and others, 1982; Peters and Zaidel, 1981).

Concrete Operations. At 6 to 8 years, children begin dealing with more
complex relations of representations, such as what Piaget (1970) called concrete operations. The nature of the difference between these relations and those
in the previous level has not been settled, but the later one clearly involves
more complex relations than the earlier one. Although some neo-Piagetian
theorists do not designate this as a separate level (Case, 1980), many abilities
do seem to spurt in this age period (Siegler, 1978; White, 1970). In general,
children become capable of joining multiple representations in complex constructs rather than merely relating one representation to another. For example, in the conservation of an amount of liquid, children not only relate the
height and width of a container of water to produce a concept of total amount,
but they also relate the amount in one container to that in another—a complex
set of relations. Similarly, they can attribute multiple, simultaneous emotions
to two people interacting with each other (Hand, 1981; Harter, 1982).

Beginning Formal Operations. Piaget (1970) stated that the formal
operational stage emerges between 10 and 12 years of age, and subsequent
research has found strong evidence for developmental spurts during this
period. The preadolescent develops the capacity to deal with abstractions or
hypothetical ideas, such as justice, nonconformity, and possibility. Of course,
these ideas are built upon the foundation of the concrete representations of the
previous level. For example, the concept of law at the previous level is defined
by the enumeration of concrete instances of laws: "You can't break windows,
and you can't steal." At the level that begins formal operations, children
understand a general definition integrating those instances such as: "A law is a
rule for keeping order among people" (Adelson, 1972). According to several
theories, the reorganization occurring at this point is greater than that of most
of the other levels, perhaps analogous in scope to the emergence of representation at 2 years of age. One hypothesis is that it begins a new series of reorganizations (Case, 1980; Fischer, 1980).

Later Formal Operations. Many researchers have come to believe that the formal operational level emerging at 10 to 12 years of age is not the end of the story. For example, few children at that age can pass most of Piaget's formal operations tasks. Research strongly supports at least one additional reorganization, occurring at approximately 14 to 16 years of age. Adolescents are able to relate several abstractions and to deal with the majority of Piaget's formal operations tasks at this age. Indeed, there is good evidence for developmental spurts during this age period, as shown on both Piaget's tasks and other tests of abstractions (Fischer and others, forthcoming; Martarano, 1977). These new abilities include relating arithmetic concepts (such as addition and subtraction) and coordinating political concepts (such as liberal and conservative).

Additional levels have been hypothesized beyond this age period (Biggs and Collis, 1982; Case, 1980; Commons and others, forthcoming; Fischer, 1980). Research clearly supports the existence of continuing cognitive growth after 16 years of age, but the data remain insufficient to determine whether there are further periods of discontinuity in behavioral change.

The Collaboration of Child and Environment

The concept of stage has been strongly tied with genetic or nativist approaches to development in the history of the field. Many scholars have automatically assumed that if child development occurs in stages, then those stages are somehow directly programmed by genes. But the research described in this sourcebook does not support any simple nativist view. Indeed, the framework of developmental levels presented here is expressly intended to avoid any such nativist interpretations. It fits firmly within the modern transactional or epigenetic approach, which emphasizes that all behavioral development arises from a collaboration between the child and the environment (Gottlieb, 1983). The chapter by Bullock in this sourcebook applies this approach to developmental levels, spelling out how the child and his or her environment join to produce social and cognitive development.

Where Is a Developmental Level? In using the concept of developmental level, one can still make a common error that naturally leads down the nativist path. It is easy to treat a developmental level as a characteristic of the individual child: For example, 5-year-old Jason is at the level of simple relations of representations, while 6-year-old Nicole is at the level of concrete operations. Such descriptions certainly do capture something about the behavior of each of these children, but they also hide a number of important, implicit assumptions about the environment in which each child is assessed.

One good reason to replace the concept of stage is that each child is typically characterized in terms of a monolithic stage. Research has shown repeatedly, however, that children never fit a single stage, such as concrete operations (Biggs and Collis, 1982; Feldman, 1980; Fischer, 1980; Flavell, 1983; Hand, 1981). Instead, they can be capable of demonstrating concrete-operational skills in certain domains under certain environmental conditions. To say that Nicole is at the *level* of concrete operations means that under environmental conditions that support optimal performance in certain specific domains with which Nicole has had extensive experience, she will perform at the level of concrete operations. In other domains or under other conditions, she will perform at one of the lower developmental levels. Indeed, according to the argument made by Bullock (this volume), she may even function effectively at a higher developmental level, such as formal operations, under conditions where adults provide specific support for such functioning. The child alone, then, should not be characterized as possessing a developmental level. What really possesses a level is some particular combination of the child and his or her environment.

Levels in Brain Development. Another error that often leads to nativist assumptions arises from consideration of the relationship between brain changes and cognitive-developmental levels. When a change in a brain characteristic is found to be related to a cognitive level, the brain change is often treated as a biological prerequisite necessary for the cognitive level. Brain characteristics are considered to be somehow more fundamental than behavioral characteristics, although the brain change may not occur temporally or causally prior to the cognitive level.

For example, Figure 2 presents some data that can be given a nativist interpretation. Matousek and Petersen (1973) measured the brain waves of Swedish subjects ranging from 1 to 21 years of age. Fischer and Pipp (forthcoming) used these data to examine the change with age in the relative energy of alpha waves in the occipital-parietal region, in which the developmental change measured by an electroencephalogram appears the strongest. The researchers predicted that there would be spurts in brainwave changes associated with each of the cognitive-developmental levels that fell within the age range tested. Their predictions were strongly confirmed for the spurts at the ages specified in the fourth-through-eighth levels listed in Table 1. An additional spurt at 18 to 20 years had been predicted on the basis of a hypothesized ninth level and was also supported by the evidence. That is, the results showed spurts in brainwave change at roughly the following ages: 2, 4, 8, 12, 15, and 19 years.

These data show an impressive correlation between the modal ages for the developmental levels and the ages of spurts in brainwave changes. They do not prove in any way, however, that the brain changes produced the cognitive changes. Indeed, some of the brainwave spurts clearly occur later than the cognitive spurts. For example, cognitive spurts occur as early as 5 ½ or 6 years of age for the level associated with the brainwave spurt at 8 years. Similarly, cognitive spurts occur as early as 10 years for the level associated with the brainwave spurt at 12 years. From these data, a sensible hypothesis would be that children first develop the capacity to behave at each of these levels, and

Figure 2. A Series of Developmental Spurts
in the Electroencephalogram

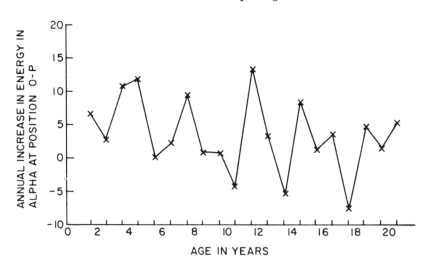

AGE IN YEARS

* The EEG was measured in the occipital-parietal region, and the percentage of energy was calculated by dividing the amount of energy in alpha by the total amount of energy in all waves (John, 1977).

Source: Data taken from Matousek and Petersen, 1973.

then a change in their brain produces the brainwave spurt. The brain changes related to each developmental level could certainly be induced by some behavioral event. Then, presumably, the brain change would allow the child to construct behaviors more easily at the level. A less substantive relationship between behavior and the brain could also explain the data in Figure 2. An individual's state of arousal has a strong effect on brain waves. If the emergence of a new cognitive level led to a generally increased state of arousal, then the arousal could in turn lead to a change in brain waves.

Undoubtedly the brain plays an important role in the emergence of each developmental level. Nevertheless, finding a brainwave correlate of a developmental level should lead to neither a nativist interpretation nor an assumption that the brain event in any way precedes the emergence of the level. Both the characteristics of the child and environmental factors always combine in the production of a cognitive level.

Summary and Conclusions

Developmental research has not supported the classic concept of stage, but a recasting of the concept in terms of developmental level shows great promise. Level is a transactional concept for explaining the contributions of both the child and his or her environment to the broad changes in children's behavior between birth and early adulthood. Under certain environmental condi-

18

tions, especially those producing optimal performance, discontinuities in the speed of development seem to occur—that is, spurts or other abrupt changes in the developmental function for a behavior. These discontinuities are generally associated with certain age periods, at least for middle-class children.

A developmental level is characterized by a cluster of discontinuities within a restricted age period for each individual child, under certain environmental conditions. The discontinuities come and go as a function of the conditions of assessment. An overview of the research on developmental discontinuities indicates that eight successive levels occur between the ages of 2 months and 16 years. In general, discontinuity promises to be a new and useful criterion for developmental change that can replace the unsuccessful empiricalcriteria, such as synchrony, traditionally applied in stage theories.

References

Adelson, J. "The Political Imagination of the Adolescent." In J. Kagan and R. Coles (Eds.), *Twelve to Sixteen: Early Adolescence*. New York: Norton, 1972.

Biggs, J., and Collis, K. *A System for Evaluating Learning Outcomes: The SOLO Taxonomy.* New York: Academic Press, 1982.

Broughton, J. M. "Piaget's Structural Developmental Psychology. III. Function and the Problem of Knowledge." *Human Development,* 1981, *24,* 257–285.

Case, R. "The Underlying Mechanism of Intellectual Development." In J. R. Kirby and J. B. Gibbs (Eds.), *Cognition, Development, and Instruction.* New York: Academic Press, 1980.

Colby, A., Kohlberg, L., Gibbs, J., and Lieberman, M. "A Longitudinal Study of Moral Judgment." *Monographs of the Society for Research in Child Development,* 1983, *48* (1), entire issue.

Commons, M., Richards, R., and Kuhn, D. "Metasystematic Reasoning." In M. Commons, F. Richards, and C. Armon (Eds.), *Beyond Formal Operations.* New York: Praeger, forthcoming.

Emde, R., Gaensbauer, T., and Harmon, R. "Emotional Expression in Infancy: A Biobehavioral Study." *Psychological Issues,* 1976, *10* (37).

Epstein, H. "Growth Spurts During Brain Development: Implications for Educational Policy and Practice." In J. S. Chall and A. F. Mirsky (Eds.), *Education and the Brain.* Chicago: University of Chicago Press, 1978.

Feldman, D. H. *Beyond Universals in Cognitive Development.* Norwood, N.J.: Ablex, 1980.

Fischer, K. W. "A Theory of Cognitive Development: The Control and Construction of Hierarchies of Skills." *Psychological Review,* 1980, *87,* 477–531.

Fischer, K. W. "Human Cognitive Development in the First Four Years." *The Behavioral and Brain Sciences,* 1982, *5,* 282–283.

Fischer, K. W. "Illuminating the Processes of Moral Development: A Commentary." *Monographs of the Society for Research in Child Development,* 1983, *48,* 97–107. See Colby above.

Fischer, K. W., and Bullock, D. "Patterns of Data: Sequence, Synchrony, and Constraint in Cognitive Development." In K. W. Fischer (Ed.), *Cognitive Development.* New Directions for Child Development, no. 12. San Francisco: Jossey-Bass, 1981.

Fischer, K. W., and Pipp, S. L. "Processes of Cognitive Development: Optimal Level and Skill Acquisition." In R. J. Sternberg (Ed.), *Mechanisms of Cognitive Development.* San Francisco: Freeman, forthcoming.

Fischer, K. W., Pipp, S. L., and Bullock, D. "Detecting Discontinuities in Development: Method and Measurement." In R. Harmon and R. N. Emde (Eds.), *Continuities and Discontinuities in Development.* New York: Plenum, forthcoming.

Flavell, J. H. "Structures, Stages, and Sequences in Cognitive Development." In W. A. Collins (Ed.), *Minnesota Symposium on Child Psychology.* Hillsdale, N.J.: Erlbaum, 1983.

Fuson, K. C., Richards, J., and Briars, D. J. "The Acquisition and Elaboration of the Number Word Sequence." In C. Brainerd (Ed.), *Children's Logical and Mathematical Cognition.* New York: Springer-Verlag, 1982.

Gottlieb, G. "The Psychobiological Approach to Developmental Issues." In P. H. Mussen (Eds.), *Handbook of Child Psychology.* Vol. 1. New York: Wiley, 1983.

Halford, G. S. *The Development of Thought.* Hillsdale, N.J.: Erlbaum, 1982.

Hand, H. H. "The Relation Between Developmental Level and Spontaneous Behavior: The Importance of Sampling Contexts." In K. W. Fischer (Ed.), *Cognitive Development.* New Directions for Child Development, no. 12. San Francisco: Jossey-Bass, 1981.

Harter, S. "A Cognitive-Developmental Approach to Children's Use of Affect and Trait Labels." In F. Serafica (Ed.), *Social-Cognitive Development in Context.* New York: Guilford Press, 1982.

John, E. R. *Functional Neuroscience: Neurometrics.* Hillsdale, N.J.: Erlbaum, 1977.

Kohlberg, L. "Stage and Sequence: The Cognitive-Developmental Approach to Socialization." In D. Goslin (Ed.), *Handbook of Socialization Theory and Research.* Chicago: Rand McNally, 1969.

McCall, R. B. "Qualitative Transitions in Behavioral Development in the First Two Years of Life." In M. H. Bornstein and W. Kessen (Eds.), *Psychological Development from Infancy.* Hillsdale, N.J.: Erlbaum, 1979.

Martarano, S. C. "A Developmental Analysis of Performance on Piaget's Formal Operations Tasks." *Developmental Psychology,* 1977, *13*, 666-672.

Matousek, M., and Petersen, I. "Frequency Analysis of the EEG in Normal Children and Adolescents." In P. Kellaway and I. Petersen (Eds.), *Automation of Clinical Electroencephalography.* New York: Raven Press, 1973.

Peters, A. M., and Zaidel, E. "The Acquisition of Homonymy." *Cognition,* 1981, *8*, 187-207.

Piaget, J. "Logique et Équilibre dans les Comportements du Sujet." *Études d'Épistémologie Génétique,* 1957, *2*, 27-118.

Piaget, J. "Piaget's Theory." In P. H. Mussen (Ed.), *Carmichael's Manual of Child Psychology.* New York: Wiley, 1970.

Rubin, K. H. "Egocentrism in Childhood: A Unitary Construct?" *Child Development,* 1973, *44*, 102-110.

Seibert, J. M., Hogan, A. E., and Mundy, P. C. "Mental Age and Cognitive Stage in Very Young Handicapped Children." *Intelligence,* in press.

Siegler, R. S. "The Origins of Scientific Reasoning." In R. S. Siegler (Ed.), *Children's Thinking: What Develops?* Hillsdale, N.J.: Erlbaum, 1978.

Siegler, R. S. "Developmental Sequences Within and Between Concepts." *Monographs of the Society for Research in Child Development,* 1981, *46*, entire issue.

Uzgiris, I. C. "Organization of Sensorimotor Intelligence." In M. Lewis (Ed.), *Origins of Intelligence: Infancy and Early Childhood.* New York: Plenum, 1976.

Wallon, H. *De l'Acte à la Pensée. [From Action to Thought].* Paris: Flammarion, 1970.

Werner, H. "The Concept of Development from a Comparative and Organismic Point of View." In D. B. Harris (Ed.), *The Concept of Development.* Minneapolis: University of Minnesota Press, 1957.

White, S. H. "Some General Outlines of the Matrix of Developmental Changes Between Five and Seven Years." *Bulletin of the Orton Society,* 1970, *20*, 41-57.

Wohlwill, J. F. *The Study of Behavioral Development.* New York: Academic Press, 1973.

Kurt W. Fischer is associate professor of psychology at the University of Denver and director of the Cognitive Development Laboratory. His interests include the nature of developmental change and the relations among social, cognitive, emotional and physical development.

Contrary to the traditional portrait of physical growth as a gradual, continuous process, infants seem to grow in episodic spurts. Their behavior tends to develop in a similar discontinuous manner, with biobehavioral shifts occurring at 2 and 8 months of age.

Episodic Growth in Infancy: A Preliminary Report on Length, Head Circumference, and Behavior

Michelle Lampl
Robert N. Emde

The relation between physical growth and behavioral development is a central issue in the study of development. The investigation of this relationship has been stymied, however, by apparent incompatibilities between the nature of change in the two domains. Research on behavioral development has shown important discontinuities, including biobehavioral shifts in early infancy (Emde and others, 1976). Physical growth, on the other hand, usually is considered to be a continuous process of slow and steady deceleration from early infancy to mid childhood. Consequently, the findings of previous research on the relation between growth and behavioral development have been difficult to interpret (for example, Lasky and others, 1981). We believe the assumption

Partial support for this research was provided by the Developmental Psychobiology Research Group Endowment Fund of the Department of Psychiatry, University of Colorado Medical School, provided by the Grant Foundation; and from National Institute of Mental Health Grants MH22803 and Research Scientist Award, KO5 MH36808 to Dr. Emde. The first author would like to acknowledge the statistical assistance of Paul Shaman and express appreciation to Alex Roche, Sol Katz, and Frank Johnston for their advice during the course of this research.

K. W. Fischer (Ed.). *Levels and Transitions in Children's Development.* New Directions for Child Development, no. 21. San Francisco: Jossey-Bass, September 1983.

that physical growth is continuous needs to be reexamined. There may well be discontinuities in growth, just as there are discontinuities in behavioral development. This chapter addresses the question of whether there are discontinuities in physical growth in infancy and presents a preliminary analysis of data from one of our studies.

The Assumption of Continuity in Early Growth and the Background for the Present Research

Postnatal growth is characterized in current descriptions as an orderly process that occurs at a slow and steady pace. From the early postnatal months to adolescence, the velocity of growth gradually decreases, with one period of acceleration between the ages of 7 and 9 years and another during adolescence (Tanner and Cameron, 1980; Tanner and others, 1966). Although researchers have often speculated about "waves" of growth (that is, periods of acceleration followed by deceleration), the general consensus has been that such an episodic process is probably no more than an epiphenomenon of measurement error.

Most developmentalists believe that early growth shows linear change (Johnston, 1978). We felt, however, that this assumption needed examination through a close look at growth during infancy. Assessed at frequent intervals, would such growth demonstrate a linear function—or would it be uneven? Furthermore, would growth rates correspond to important phenomena in behavioral development? The background for these questions can be found in two recent research trends in developmental psychobiology.

The first trend is based on a general multidisciplinary view that development is not simply linear, cumulative, or additive. This is not merely the latest fashion in the old theoretical controversy of connectivity versus epigenesis, or continuity versus discontinuity. Now there are empirical data documenting the form of developmental change.

Studies that look closely at cognitive development show that spurts and dips occur at certain ages, and this pattern is also true for language development (see the chapters in this sourcebook; Bever, 1982; McCall, 1979; Mehler, 1982). Unevenness is even more obvious in early motor development, although researchers previously have failed to appreciate the significance of uneven rates of change, such as those highlighted long ago in McGraw's studies (1945). Now there is a resurgence of interest in observing motor development closely and in understanding mechanisms that underlie regressions, spurts, and restructurings in growth (Prechtl, 1982).

Data from the neurosciences probably emphasize discontinuities in development most dramatically. Experimental work with nonhuman primates and other mammals as well as neurological observations with humans reveal a remarkable unevenness in the development of neural functions. Furthermore, such functional developments are accompanied by structural change. For example, there is remodeling of synaptic network structures in the development of the primate visual system and the cerebellum (Rakic, 1977). Apparently synapses are overproduced in the brain early in development, with a selective survival of some that depends partly on experience (Greenough and Schwark, 1983). The number of synapses in the frontal cortex of a human child at 1 to 2 years is reported to be 50 percent more than the normal adult number (Huttenlocher, 1979): Clearly, neurons and groups of neurons die in the course of neurogenesis. Correspondingly, transient neural reflex patterns are known to appear and reappear in development. Earlier Jacksonian explanations (Jackson, 1958) for these disappearances—that they occur through a simple inhibition by the gradual development of higher neural centers—no longer seem tenable. Among the reasons for this shift in thinking is the observed unevenness in functioning over the course of development. Clearly, the neurosciences give us a dynamic picture of restructuring and change during development. It is important, therefore, to re-assess whether physical growth corresponds to this unevenness in functioning or is linear.

The second trend in developmental psychobiology which has fueled the research to be presented here is based on data from longitudinal studies, which have produced a growing appreciation that development is not continuous in any simple sense. These studies have found that stabilities in behavior across the first two postnatal years are difficult to document, whether temperament (Plomin, 1983) or the effects of early experience (Clarke and Clarke, 1977; Emde, 1981; Kagan and others, 1979) are measured. In addition, results from longitudinal studies have led to more information about the actual timing of shifts—that is, ages when there is a reorganization of behavior across multiple domains (for example, in perceptual, cognitive, emotional, and social organization).

Programmatic research on such shifts carried out at the University of Colorado School of Medicine (Emde and others, 1976) provided impetus for Rene Spitz's *Genetic Field Theory of Ego Formation* (1959), which postulates several periods of qualitative change during the first two years of life. Spitz discusses these in terms of "psychic organizers," which are indicated by the onset of affective changes (smiling, 8-month-old anxiety, and the semantic "no" gesture). As a result of our studies, we confirmed that major qualitative changes in infancy occur at 2 months and 7 to 9 months, not only across several behavioral domains but also in areas of central nervous system electrophysiology (the electroencephalogram and sleep state organization) and autonomic nervous system regulation (heart rate changes). Because these areas of qualitative change include biology as well as behavior and because a strong maturational factor appears to be important, we designated such discontinuities as normative times of "biobehavioral shift." Other convergent evidence also supports these first-year normative times of shift, taken from investigators working from quite different theoretical perspectives, and these researchers' data also demonstrate other normative times of shift in the second year: at 12 to 13 and 18 to 21 months of age (see chapters in this sourcebook by McCall and Corrigan, Zelazo and Leonard; McCall, 1979; Kagan and others, 1979; Uzgiris, 1976; Zelazo, 1982).

Therefore, with this theoretical and research background in mind, we have formulated several hypotheses. First, we asserted that physical growth during the first postnatal year would not correspond to a simple linear function (that is, show a constant negative velocity, or deceleration), but would evidence unevenness or spurts instead. Second, we believed that there would be a specificity to this unevenness, with spurts in growth corresponding to the previously documented times of biobehavioral shifts at 2 months and at 7 to 9 months. Our third hypothesis is more speculative, considering our primary emphasis on growth measurements: If such spurts exist for growth, they correspond to significant developmental changes in behavior, whether or not the changes occur at the times of biobehavioral shift. Such correspondence should be most prominent with growth spurts in head circumference.

The Present Study

The infants in this study were recruited through mothers in prenatal Lamaze classes. The sample population was a highly select and nonrandom population of lower- to upper-middle class whites. A total of twenty-eight infants (eighteen females and ten males) was observed weekly or semiweekly for varying lengths of time during the first year of life. All infants were initially assessed by 3 weeks of age. The entire sample was seen until 4 months of age, twenty-one infants were seen until 6 months, seventeen infants until 9 months, and nine infants until 12 months. Infants were selected for inclusion in the study according to the following birth criteria: birth weight greater than or equal to 2500 grams, 38 to 42 weeks gestational age, uncomplicated pregnancies and deliveries, and one- and five-minute Apgar scores for cardiorespiratory states between 8 and 10. (The highest possible Apgar score is 10). In addition, none were subsequently diagnosed as having any physical problems during their first year. All infants lived in Denver, Colorado, an environment which is approximately one mile above sea level.

The physical growth of the infants was assessed through anthropometric measurements according to standard techniques (Weiner and Lourie, 1969), taken weekly on the entire sample of twenty-eight infants and twice weekly on a subsample of eighteen infants. All data were collected through home visits that were scheduled at the convenience of the parents, with attention paid to the changing schedule of their babies. Physical growth measurements were taken within one hour of the same time at each visit, to control for any diurnal variation that might exist.

The behavioral development of the infants was investigated by several methods. Parents were asked to keep daily written records on their infants, which included keeping track of sleep, eating, and illness episodes. For behavioral observations, they were asked to write down anything they would want to tell their spouse, parent, or best friend about their child. Parental records were augmented by participant observations made by one of the investigators. Extensive notes were taken at each visit, including observations of the infant's behavioral state and development as well as information regarding the social and nonsocial environment. This ethnographic approach can produce rich contextual details that when combined with the systematic observations of behavioral development, nutritional intake, sleep, and growth, provide a basis for more focused studies in the future. No standard behavioral assessment scale was used because of the exploratory nature of the research.

Physical Growth Data

Anthropometric techniques were used to measure body length and head circumference (Weiner and Lourie, 1969). The investigator served as a rater in all sessions, and once a week an independent rater took measurements for assessment of interrater reliability. Each rater took two measurements (called "replicates") on every occasion, and the average of the two measurements served as data. Only the investigator's measurements were used for the analyses reported here.

Following the standard approach to the assessment of anthropometric measurement error, the technical errors of measurement were calculated for inter- and intraobserver reliability of measurement (Johnston and others, 1974; Tanner, 1963; Utermohle and Zegura, 1982; Zavaleta and Malina, 1982). Based on 224 measurements, interobserver replicate measurement error was 1.2 mm for length and 0.56 mm for head circumference, and inter-observer reliability was high ($r = .95$ for length, .98 for head circumference).

The error variance of replicate measurements was significantly different between children. Therefore, in this preliminary analysis, each infant's growth data have been individually analyzed, and growth measurements have been assessed with respect to the reliability of measurement derived from his or her own replicate measurements. (For a complete discussion of measurement reliability, see Lampl, 1983). For the initial display of data, the increment method of analysis was chosen in which the change in length or head circumference from one session to the next was analyzed. A major requirement of the increment method is establishment of confidence intervals for measurement error (van der Linden and others, 1970). Any growth increments that exceed the 99 percent level of measurement error are considered reliable and independent of measurement error.

Results: A Close Look Reveals Episodic Rather Than Linear Growth

The generally accepted linear model for normal growth has been developed from studies where individuals were measured at annual, biannual, or monthly intervals. Figure 1 presents standard growth charts based on this

26

Figure 1. Susan's Data Plotted Monthly on Traditional Growth Charts

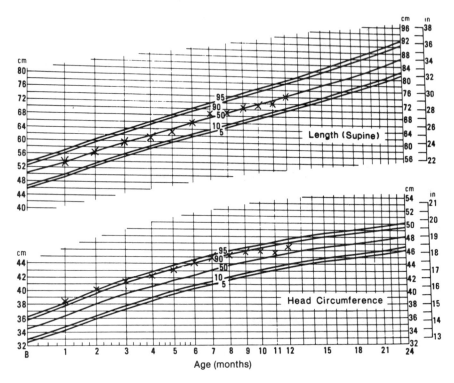

Note: Susan's data are indicated by the X's on the graph. The solid lines designate the 5th, 10th, 50th, 90th, and 95th percentiles of each variable according to the NCHS Growth Charts.

model. Monthly data from one representative female infant in our study, Susan, have been superimposed on the charts. These graphs show an infant's total length and head circumference instead of increments. Figure 2 illustrates a velocity curve, in which the same data are plotted as quarterly increments through the first year.

A different picture of normal growth emerges when one takes a closer look, using twice-weekly measurements and increment analysis. Figures 3 and 4 illustrate incremental growth in length and head circumference for Susan. Age in postnatal weeks is plotted on the x-axis, and the increments are indicated in millimeters along the y-axis. Each histogram bar represents a change in either length or head circumference during a time period of one-half week.

Length. For the measurements taken on Susan, the 95 percent confidence interval was 3.0 mm, and the 99 percent interval was 4.0 mm. Changes which exceed these limits are considered significant, and all measurement

Figure 2. Susan's Growth Velocity Plotted Quarterly

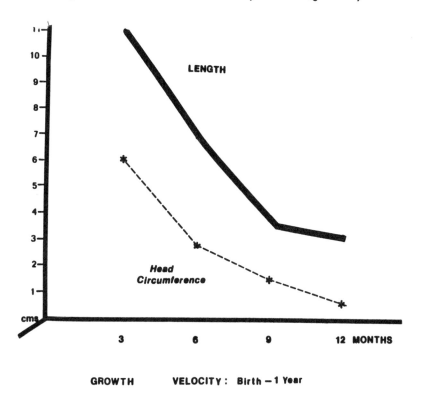

GROWTH   VELOCITY : Birth — 1 Year

differences that fall below these lines are assumed to be associated with errors of measurement. A number of times during her first year, Susan showed increments of between 10.0 and 12.0 mm during half a week: at weeks 5, 9, 11, 22, 43, and 46, as shown in Figure 3. In addition, a number of smaller, significant increments occurred at other ages, and these were separated by plateau periods of insignificant or little growth.

Although these increments could possibly have been due to an artifact of the preceding decrements, this interpretation seems unlikely for several reasons. First, the method of assessing error in incremental data took into consideration the dependent and negatively correlated nature of these data. Second, there were 35 episodes of increments that were significant beyond the 99 percent confidence limit, while there were only 5 equally significant decrements. Nonetheless, these decrements could have influenced the results if they reflected an overestimation at the measurement point preceding the decrement or an underestimation at the point of the decrement. To adjust for this possi-

Figure 3. Susan's Growth in Length Measured Twice Weekly

LENGTH

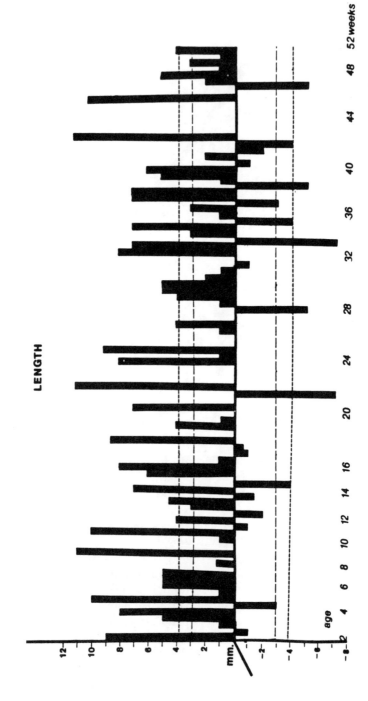

Note: The lines with large dashes parallel to the x-axis indicate the 95 percent confidence interval for measurement error, and those with small dashes indicate the 99 percent confidence interval.

Figure 4. Susan's Growth in Head Circumference Measured Twice Weekly

HEAD CIRCUMFERENCE

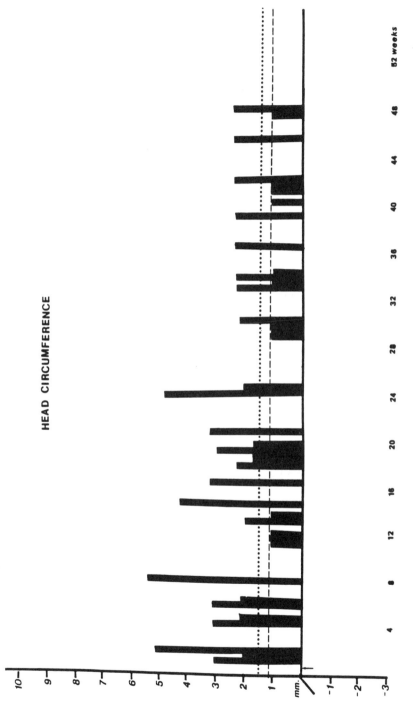

Note: The dashed line parallel to the x-axis indicates the 95 percent confidence interval for measurement error, and the dotted line indicates the 99 percent confidence interval.

bility, significant decrements were subtracted from neighboring increments. This resulted in 31 significant episodes of growth in length that still exceeded the 99 percent confidence interval for this child.

The data from a second infant, Heidi, indicate the variability in measurements between individuals. The 95 percent confidence limit of measurement error for this child was 3.6 mm, and the 99 percent limit was 4.9 mm. On two documented occasions, Heidi grew between 18 and 20 mm in length during a period of three days, once at 7 weeks and once at 47 weeks. Further growth spurts between 10.0 and 15.0 mm were documented on a number of occasions. Overall, there were 32 episodes of significant increments that were beyond the 99 percent level, while there were only 5 equally significant decrements. The most dramatic increments were not preceded by decrements. Furthermore, when the decrements were subtracted from the neighboring increments, 27 significant incremental episodes remained. Clearly, the amount and timing of the episodes showed considerable individual variability, as is illustrated by these two children.

Head Circumference. Head circumference growth showed similar episodic spurts. For Susan's measurements, as shown in Figure 4, the 95 percent confidence interval of measurement error was 1.2 mm, and the 99 percent limit was 1.5 mm. At three ages (3, 8, and 24 weeks) an increment of as much as 5.0 mm occurred during a particular three-day measurement period. Furthermore, a number of 2.0 to 3.0 mm increments occurred throughout the first year. Overall, there were 27 significant increments in head circumference beyond the 99 percent confidence level and no significant decrements.

For the second infant, Heidi, the 95 percent limit of measurement error was 2.0 mm, and the 99 percent limit was 2.6 mm. Significant increments of 5.0 to 6.0 mm were observed during weeks 2, 10, and 22, and smaller significant increments occurred during weeks 5, 6, 14, and 30. Overall, there were 11 significant increments in head circumference beyond the 99 percent level during the year and no significant decrements. The relatively high level of error associated with measurement of this infant accounts for the small number of significant increments.

These two infants illustrate the individual variability that characterized such growth patterns among the sample of twenty-eight children studied. In spite of this variability, all infants showed a patter of episodic increments in growth that clearly exceeded the error of measurement. Variability between subjects occurred in the number and in the timing of such increments, but not in the fact of their occurrence. The mean number of growth increments for the entire sample was as follows: birth to 4 months (measured twice weekly) — 10 increments in length and 8 in head circumference; birth to 1 year (measured twice weekly) — 28 increments in length and 23 in head circumference. (See Lampl, 1983, for growth data of the entire sample.) In conclusion, episodic growth occurred frequently and was independent of measurement error. Traditional protocols have not shown such growth spurts, most probably because measurements have been taken yearly, twice yearly, or at most monthly during the first year of life.

We would emphasize that the exact frequency of measurement is relatively arbitrary. Many twice-weekly increments cluster together, and bar graphs may not adequately represent the extent of rapid growth when it occurs. For example, at 20 weeks, Susan had completed an 8.0 mm increment in head circumference that occurred over the prior two weeks (see Figure 4). At 25 weeks, she had completed a 6.5 mm increment in head circumference that occurred over the prior week. Weekly measurements would detect the same periods of incremental growth, although the exact form of the graph would be somewhat different. A graph based on weekly measurement is shown for the infant John in Figure 5.

A variety of time-sampling approaches are required to best capture the growth increments for purposes of discovering underlying mechanisms of growth spurts. But these results do suggest that the traditional portrayal of physical growth should be reevaluated. Considering the body of evidence that also documents growth spurts at midchildhood and adolescence, it seems reasonable to hypothesize that the entire process of physical growth proceeds by episodic spurts.

Other Measures of Growth. In addition to the data presented above, measurements of weight as well as numerous body dimensions that reflect the fatness, size, and shape of the body were collected. Although the data have not been statistically analyzed yet, they appear to show episodic changes in all dimensions. It is well known that under adequate nutritional conditions, changes in body weight and fatness are more responsive to environmental factors such as diet, activity, and mild infection than body growth in length and head circumference. Future analyses will focus on the correlations between daily dietary intake, activity, and illness of individual infants. Growth as a process of episodic spurts probably demands a high energy intake, which would be reflected in body composition changes. Thus, there may be a common mechanism that regulates both body growth and dietary needs. The question of whether endogenous factors are primarily responsible for growth regulation remains to be answered, but we believe our data support an endogenous timing mechanism that interacts with exogenous factors.

The Relationship Between Episodic Physical Growth and Developments in Behavior

An episodic pattern of physical growth may have implications for the study of behavioral development. In the present study, behavioral observations were conducted on fifteen infants (eight girls and seven boys). These observations focused on behavioral changes that are described in the developmental literature and included in the Bayley Scales of Infant Development (Bayley, 1969). The Bayley Scales were not actually administered but were used to categorize specific behaviors as they were achieved by each infant, according to parental report and observation by the investigator. This approach was chosen so as not to limit the data collected, while at the same time providing data comparable to a standard instrument.

Figure 5. John's Growth in Head Circumference Measured Weekly

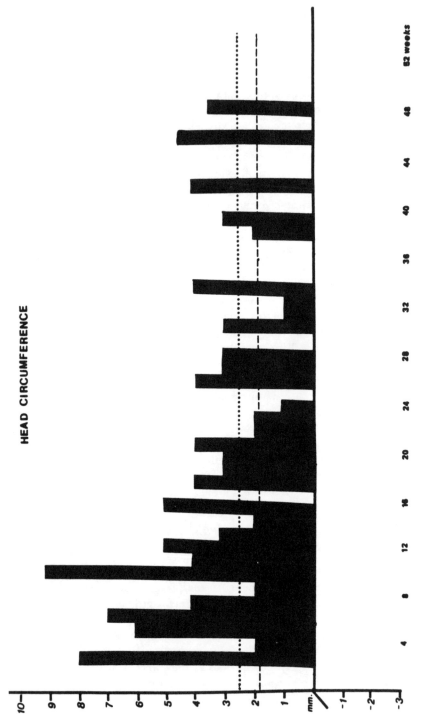

Note: The dashed line parallel to the x-axis indicates the 95 percent confidence interval for measurement error, and the dotted line indicates the 99 percent confidence interval.

Again, we will illustrate the findings with the data from Susan. Two levels of analysis will be presented. The first involves an abbreviated behavioral checklist for a few developmental milestones in motor and social and affective development: head control, hand-eye coordination in reaching, sitting, crawling, standing alone, walking, the social smile, stranger distress, separation distress, and nonstranger fearfulness. For Susan, nine of the ten motor and social and affective milestones occurred at the same time as significant head-circumference growth. The second, more intensive assessment was based on all behaviors that could be coded by the Bayley Scales of motor and mental development—a total of sixty-two items. (A list of the specific items coded is available.) These data were analyzed for occurrence of a significant increment in head circumference at the same time as a behavioral change.

During a total of ninety-eight time intervals, there were twenty-seven intervals of significant growth in head circumference. There were thirty-six intervals during which at least one behavioral item showed change. Fifty percent of the intervals containing behavioral changes also showed episodic growth in head circumference. In addition, during another 36 percent of the intervals, behavioral changes were noted within a half-week of head circumference growth. Thus, only 24 percent of the intervals with noted behavioral changes were not directly associated with growth changes. These data suggest a temporal correspondence between periodic bursts in physical growth and the onset of new behaviors. They lend encouragement to future studies exploring the biological basis for behavioral development.

Conclusion

The results provide support for our first hypothesis—that infant growth occurs unevenly, in spurts. Simple linear growth, the traditionally assumed pattern of physical development, does not seem to occur. Although we have presented detailed data from only a few infants here, all the infants studied showed multiple-growth increments in both length and head circumference that exceeded the 99 percent confidence limit. Furthermore, an additional analysis showed that the spurts in length and head circumference tend to occur together, which reinforces the proposition that spurts in growth are significant biological phenomena (Lampl, 1983).

Clearly, these findings should be replicated, and further research is called for concerning the correlates and meaning of growth spurts. From a practical standpoint alone, however, it is worth emphasizing the episodic nature of infant growth. For example, a pediatrician who encounters a large growth spurt (such as an 8.0 mm increase in head circumference in two weeks) might be alarmed falsely and suspect hydrocephalus. Research is needed to detect when such dramatic changes are clinically meaningful and when they are not. In addition, the study of growth spurts provides a major research opportunity for analyzing the mechanisms and timing of normal growth. The

34

possibility of correlating incremental growth in head circumference with maturational events, using assessments of both brain electrophysiology and behavior seems to be an exciting new direction for studies of the future.

Our second hypothesis—that there would be a concentration of unevenness in growth corresponding to the times of biobehavioral shifts at 2 and 7 to 9 months—was not supported. The illustrative cases for length and head circumference (see Figures 3, 4, and 5) do not reveal any such strong concentration. Episodic growth occurs throughout the first year, although further analyses of these and other cases might reveal some correspondence. The meaning of the apparent lack of correspondence is unclear. Perhaps physical growth spurts reflect a different maturational timetable from biobehavioral shifts, with shorter periods between spurts. Whether there is a cyclicity or particular rhythm that characterizes the growth spurts remains to be explored. Future work should also focus on the relationship between such spurts and the production of growth hormone and other diencephalic secretory events. For example, Weitzman and his colleagues (Weitzman and others, 1974) have demonstrated that many hormones under diurnal control are secreted in pulses rather than in steady fashion. Although these results involve a much shorter time frame than that of our measurements, similar processes may be involved.

Surprisingly, our third hypothesis did receive support. There seems to be a temporal correspondence between spurts in physical growth (notably in head circumference) and the onset of new behaviors. However, important questions about the specificity of this correspondence remain unanswered: Are there correspondences between growth and behavior for some behaviors and not others? Or is there a general inclination for new maturational spurts in all domains? To what extent do these spurts in head circumference reflect spurts in brain growth? Are there patterns of temporal relationship between growth spurts in head circumference, for example, and the development of particular domains of behavior? Further research must seek the answers to such questions—and to the many other questions raised by this preliminary analysis of our data.

In sum, these preliminary findings offer evidence for episodic rather than linear growth in infancy. The possibility that physical growth proceeds by episodic spurts is not only of biological interest but should also be taken into account by developmental psychobiologists. Although speculations about mechanisms regulating such a process are premature, endogenous or maturational determinants seem likely.

References

Bayley, N. *Manual for the Bayley Scales of Infant Development.* New York: The Psychological Corporation, 1969.

Bever, T. G. "Regression in the Service of Development." In T. G. Bever (Ed.), *Regressions in Mental Development: Basic Phenomena and Theories.* Hillsdale, N.J.: Erlbaum, 1982.

Clarke, A. M., and Clarke, A. D. B. *Early Experience: Myth and Evidence.* New York: Free Press, 1977.

Emde, R. N. "Changing Models of Infancy and the Nature of Early Development: Remodeling the Foundation." *Journal of the American Psychoanalytic Association,* 1981, *29,* 179–219.

Emde, R. N., Gaensbauer, T., and Harmon, R. H. *Emotional Expression in Infancy.* New York: International Universities Press, 1976.

Greenough, W. T., and Schwark, H. D. "Age-Related Aspects of Experience Effects upon Brain Structure." In R. N. Emde and R. J. Harmon (Eds.), *Continuity and Discontinuity in Development.* New York: Plenum, 1983.

Huttenlocher, P. R. "Synaptic Density in Human Frontal Cortex—Developmental Changes and Effects of Aging." *Brain Research,* 1979, *163,* 195–205.

Jackson, J. H. "Evaluation and Dissolution of the Nervous System." Reprinted in *Selected Writings of John Hughlings Jackson.* London: Stoples Press, 1958.

Johnston, F. E. "Somatic Growth of the Infant and Preschool Child." In F. Falkner and J. M. Tenner (Eds.), *Human Growth.* Vol. 2: *Postnatal Growth.* New York: Plenum, 1978.

Johnston, F. E., Hamill, P. V. V., and Lemeshow, S. *Skinfold Thickness of Youths 12–17 Years, United States.* Washington, D.C.: National Center for Health Statistics, 1974.

Kagan, J., Kearsley, R. B., and Zelazo, P. R. *Infancy: Its Place in Human Development.* Cambridge, Mass.: Harvard University Press, 1979.

Lampl, M. "Episodic Growth Patterns in the First Year of Life." Unpublished doctoral dissertation. Department of Anthropology, University of Pennsylvania, 1983.

Lasky, R. E., Klein, R. E., Yarbrough, C., Engle, P. L., Lechtig, A., and Martorell, R. "The Relationship Between Physical Growth and Infant Behavioral Development in Rural Guatemala." *Child Development,* 1981, *52,* 219–226.

McCall, R. B. "The Development of Intellectual Functioning in Infancy and the Prediction of Later I.Q." In J. D. Osofsky (Ed.), *Handbook of Infant Development.* New York: Wiley, 1979.

McGraw, M. *The Neuromuscular Maturation of the Human Infant.* New York: Columbia University Press, 1945.

Mehler, J. "Unlearning: Dips and Drops—A Theory of Cognitive Development." In T. G. Bever (Ed.), *Regressions in Mental Development: Basic Phenomena and Theories.* Hillsdale, N.J.: Erlbaum, 1982.

Plomin, R. "Childhood Temperament." In B. Lahey and A. Kazdin (Eds.), *Advances in Clinical Child Psychology,* 1983, *6,* 1–78.

Prechtl, H. F. R. "Regressions and Transformations During Neurological Development." In T. G. Bever (Ed.), *Regressions in Mental Development: Basic Phenomena and Theories.* Hillsdale, N.J.: Erlbaum, 1982.

Rakic, P. "Prenatal Development of the Visual System in Rhesus Monkeys." *Philosophical Transactions of the Royal Society of London,* 1977, *B278,* 245–260.

Spitz, R. *A Genetic Field Theory of Ego Formation: Its Implications for Pathology.* New York: International Universities Press, 1959.

Tanner, J. M. *Growth at Adolescence.* London: Blackwell Scientific, 1963.

Tanner, J. M., and Cameron, N. "Investigation of the Mid-Growth Spurt in Height, Weight, and Limb Circumference in Single-Year Velocity Data from the London 1966–67 Growth Survey." *Annals of Human Biology,* 1980, *7,* 565–577.

Tanner, J. M., Whitehouse, R. H., and Takaishi, M. "Standards from Birth to Maturity for Height, Weight, Height Velocity, and Weight Velocity: British Children, 1965 (Parts I and II)." *Archives of Disease in Childhood,* 1966, *41,* 454–471, 613–635.

Utermohle, C. J., and Zegura, S. L. "Intra- and Interobserver Error in Craniometry: A Cautionary Tale." *American Journal of Physical Anthropology,* 1982, *57,* 303–310.

Uzgiris, I. C. "Organization of Sensorimotor Intelligence." In M. Lewis (Ed.), *Origins of Intelligence.* New York: Plenum, 1976.

36

van der Linden, F. P. G. M., Hirschfeld, W. J., and Miller, R. L. "On the Presentation of Longitudinally Collected Growth Data." *Growth*, 1970, *34*, 385-400.

Weiner, J. S., and Lourie, J. A. *Human Biology: A Guide to Field Methods.* International Biological Programme Handbook, no. 9. Philadelphia: Davis, 1969.

Weitzman, E. D., Nogeire, C., Perlow, M., Fukushima, D., Sassin, J., McGregor, P., Gallagher, T. F., and Hellman, L. "Effects of a Prolonged Three-Hour Sleep-Wake Cycle on Sleep Stages, Plasma Cortisol, Growth Hormone, and Body Temperature in Man." *Journal of Clinical Endocrinology*, 1974, *38*, 1018-1030.

Zavelata, A. N., and Malina, R. M. "Growth and Body Composition of Mexican-American Boys 9 Through 14 Years of Age." *American Journal of Physical Anthropology*, 1969, *57*, 261-271.

Zelazo, P. R. "The Year-Old Infant: A Period of Major Cognitive Change." In T. G. Bever (Ed.), *Regressions in Mental Development: Basic Phenomena and Theories.* Hillsdale, N.J.: Erlbaum, 1982.

Michelle Lampl is an anthropologist working at the University of Pennsylvania and the Health Sciences Center of the University of Colorado. Her research focuses on the nature of physical growth in infancy and its relation to behavioral development.

Robert N. Emde is professor of psychiatry at the Health Sciences Center at the University of Colorado. His interests include biobehavioral shifts and emotional development in infancy.

The qualitative changes in behavior that occur between about 8 and 12 months extend to virtually all areas of development and imply that the infant undergoes a major cognitive metamorphosis at 1 year of age.

The Dawn of Active Thought

Philip R. Zelazo
Elizabeth L. Leonard

Despite the virtually unparalleled changes that occur toward the end of the first year of life, relatively little research has focused on the identification of the basis for these developmental changes. As a child nears his first birthday, his first words appear and he takes his first steps, begins to use objects as adults do, and reacts with distress and protest when left with a stranger in an unfamiliar place. At 12 months of age, children also begin to react to information processing tasks in ways that imply a cognitive reorganization that may form the basis for these changes (Zelazo, 1979, 1982b). The behavioral changes range from gross and fine motor to linguistic, social, and cognitive activities. These remarkably consistent changes across domains occurring in a relatively short time span define one of the clearest qualitative transitions in development. Indeed, the change in behavior from 8 to 12 months of age is so extensive that is seems to show a cognitive metamorphosis. What underlies this change from a nonverbal, relatively fearless, crawling infant that mouths,

Much of the research presented in this article and the time required to prepare it was supported by grants from the Office of Special Education (#6007603979) to Philip Zelazo and Richard Kearsley and The Carnegie Corporation of New York to Philip Zelazo. We wish to thank Marguerite Randolph for her valuable assistance with this research and Jerome Kagan for focusing attention on the cognitive changes occurring toward the end of the first year. Of course, we accept full responsibility for the views expressed here.

K. W. Fischer (Ed.). *Levels and Transitions in Children's Development.* New Directions for Child Development, no. 21. San Francisco: Jossey-Bass, September 1983.

waves, and bangs objects indiscriminately to a young person who uses words, fears strangers and unfamiliar places, walks upright, and uses the objects of his culture appropriately? What factors permit this increase in both the specificity and diversity of the year-old child's behavior?

The precise mechanisms underlying this change remain to be explained through future research, but one aspect appears clear: The year-old infant behaves as though he or she can generate specific ideas for specific situations with relative rapidity. This rapid generation of ideas can account for the transformation of behaviors across several domains. Many psychologists acknowledge that the development of central processing ability may dictate a readiness for certain changes, the expression of which is dependent upon appropriate environmental opportunities for practicing new behaviors (Fischer, 1980; Fischer and Bullock, 1981; Kagan and others, 1978; Zelazo, 1979, 1982b; Zelazo and others, in press). And as Fischer suggests (1980), extending cognitive research and theory beyond the study of the acquisition of knowledge to linguistic, social, and behavioral competencies may explain some of the mysteries of early development. The behavioral metamorphosis that takes place in a year-old child agrees with the criteria outlined by Fischer for the modified concept of stage that he calls an optimal level. The data presented here were not derived as a specific test of the optimal-level hypothesis, but they appear to support it.

In this chapter we will attempt to demonstrate that the behavioral changes occurring toward the end of the first year are genuine developmental transformations. In addition, it appears that there is high interval synchrony (the development of two or more new performance capabilities within a limited time frame) among the many new behaviors emerging during this transition.

We used the hypothetico-deductive method to test the prediction that the new behaviors have their origin in a qualitative change in central processing capacity. Two strategies for evaluation of this prediction were employed in our research. First, we hypothesized a specific explanatory construct—the capacity to generate ideas rapidly—to account for observed results from our own studies. Implications for different domains of development were derived from this construct and tested in our laboratory. A second strategy for evaluating the nature of the developmental change was to test implications of the explanatory construct against findings from past research. In cases where existing data were reexamined, two criteria for evaluating the ages at which changes occurred were followed: (1) Only behaviors that showed statistically significant increases in frequency were considered admissible. (2) Only actively expressive positive or negative behaviors, such as smiling or crying, were used; behaviors such as wariness or watching have ambiguous meanings and thus were excluded from consideration.

Despite the shortcomings of data collected for other purposes in past studies, the consistency in findings is clear. It is not until about 12 months of age that the new behaviors occur reliably, lending support to the notion that a cognitive metamorphosis may set the stage for the year-old infant's behavioral changes. If the end of the first year marks the dawn of active thought, then it is likely that this cognitive change has a strong maturational component. Enormous variability in caretaking approaches occurs naturally, and the resulting normal variation in opportunities for practice may contribute to the variability in age of onset of some behaviors. However, the cognitive change sets the lower limit for age of onset.

Processing Nonsocial Stimuli

The study of attention during infancy has revealed the infant's capacity to create memories for visual and auditory events (Cohen and Gelber, 1975; Fagan, 1978; Lewis, 1970; McCall and Kagan, 1967; Zelazo, 1979). Moreover, one of the procedures used to study infant attention—the habituation-dishabituation procedure—implies elementary information-processing abilities. In the habituation paradigm, a stimulus such as a vertical array of X's and Y's is presented repeatedly for a fixed number of trials or until a decrease occurs in looking (or some other response). Following habituation, a different stimulus—for example the same array of X's and Y's in an oblique orientation—is introduced and usually produces renewed attention, called dishabituation. In order for infants to display habituation and dishabituation, they must process and respond to the standard sensory information, hold that information in memory, and retrieve it for comparison with the dishabituating stimulus. Also, two additional propositions follow from this analysis. First, infants appear to have the capacity to create internal representations of events—that is, to build memories. Second, the creation of memories may involve, but need not require, gross and fine motor actions.

Data collected in several studies that used a variation of the habituation-disbahituation procedure (from the Standard-Transformation-Return paradigm) imply that changes in information-processing ability occur toward the end of a child's first year. A series of sequential visual or auditory events were presented and repeated so that children's capacities to develop expectancies could be assessed (Kagan and others, 1978; Zelazo, 1979). In each series, the standard stimulus was presented for a fixed number of trials. Then a discrepant variation of this stimulus (called the transformation) was presented and repeated, followed by the reappearance and repetition of the standard. Six series of events were used: three auditory and three visual sequences. Two visual sequences are described below to illustrate the nature of the procedure and the manner in which responses to these procedures forecast the cognitive metamorphosis at 1 year of age.

In the cube sequence, a two-inch orange wooden cube was lifted out of a blue box and moved in a fixed "N" pattern for six trials (Zelazo and others, 1975). On the seventh through ninth trials, either a moderately discrepant or a novel object was presented, followed by the reappearance of the standard stimulus for three additional trials. Infants in the "moderately discrepant" group viewed a one-and-a-half-inch cube that was identical to the standard except for size; the "novel" group of infants watched a one-and-a-half-inch yellow, rippled plastic cylinder that bore no relation to the standard. In the light sequence (Zelazo, 1982b), children watched the presenter's hand lift a rod through a 240-degree arc and touch the first of three brightly colored bulbs. All the bulbs lighted for four seconds before the presenter's hand returned the rod to the starting position and disappeared from view. During the transformation trials, children in the "no rod" group watched the hand come out and the lights go on without the movement of the rod. During a second moderately discrepant, "disordered" transformation, all the components of the light stimulus were retained, but in a markedly different sequence: The rod moved through the arc without the aid of the hand, touched the bulbs momentarily but did not light them on contact; instead, the bulbs were lighted upon the return of the rod to the starting position. The lights remained on for four seconds and went off with the reappearance of the hand hovering over the bulbs.

We conducted two sets of experiments using these two visual sequences with approximately 250 children. In one set, patterns of responsiveness to a mixed series of stimuli were examined cross-sectionally for boys and girls at 5½, 7½, 9½, and 11½ months of age, without control groups. In a second series, changes in responsiveness occurring between 9½ and 11½ months of age were examined with control groups added. Durations of looking and vocalization as well as beat-by-beat measures of heart rate served as the principal measures. Children sat on their mother's lap and observed the presentation of stimuli on an illuminated stage, resembling a puppet theater and located approximately eighteen inches in front of them.

Results

In general, visual attention to these events in the experiments increased even though other types of older infants tended to process information more rapidly and to look less. One explanation for this result—that older infants think about these sequences (Kagan, 1972)—received support from heart rate data showing acceleration to greater discrepancies between the standard and transformation stimuli, a response associated with mental effort in adults (Kahneman and others, 1969). Moreover, vocalizations increased with age and appeared to announce recognition and assimilation of minimally discrepant information at 11½ months, but not earlier. This pattern of reactivity indicates that a change in information-processing ability begins between 7½ and 9½ months and is expressed through a variety of behaviors by 11½ months—a pattern that is consistent with transitions reported using psychometric scales (McCall and others, 1977).

In the cube sequence, visual fixation increased sharply between 7½ and 9½ months with relatively stable responding before and after this change. Overall looking time was lowest at 7½ months and highest at 9½ months, a result that contradicts earlier findings. Lewis (1970) summarizes a large body of data that demonstrates that looking time spent on static visual stimuli decreases with age, a result that implies more rapid information processing in older infants. However, one possible resolution to the contradiction between our results of increased looking time and past findings is that as infants become more mature, they not only process more rapidly but bring more information to the situation. That is, older children may look longer at the cube sequence because they may be generating more ideas about this relatively complex sequence. In addition, examination of vocalizations occurring during the intertrial interval revealed increases with age through 11 ½ months, except for a decrease at 9 ½ months, precisely the point when visual fixation was highest.

Similar results were found with the light sequence. An examination of 203 children tested in the first experiment with four variations of the light discrepancy revealed a drop in vocalization to the light sequence at 9 ½ months (Zelazo, 1982b). The mean percentage of infants that vocalized per trial block to the light sequence increased linearly from 5 ½ to 7 ½ to 11 ½ months with a decrease at 9 ½ months. The data showed the same pattern for both the light and cube sequences, indicating that the decrease in vocalization at 9 ½ months is generalizable to several complex nonsocial stimuli. Heart rate changes during the discrepancy trials also were consistent with the hypothesized capacity to generate ideas. We hypothesized that if assimilation of the moderate "disordered" and "no rod" discrepancies did not occur, cardiac acceleration would occur, implying mental effort (see Kahneman and others, 1969). Mean heart rate over trial blocks for four periods of the light sequence were examined. The patterns for both the highest and lowest heart rate reactions were consistent over trial blocks. The heart rate patterns for standard and return trial blocks before and after the discrepancy period remained similar, indeed almost parallel, implying assimilation. However, heart rate to the discrepant portion of the light sequence remained high, unlike the reaction in the "no change" control condition, which indicates that the usual pattern of assimilation did not occur. It appears that infants attended to the discrepancy but did not resolve it. Thus, in the two visual sequences, all three measures—heart rate, fixation, and vocalization—supported the assumption that the year-old infant gains the capacity to generate ideas.

Vocalization and Pointing to Social Stimuli

The increased vocalization to nonsocial stimuli suggests that the assimilation of slight discrepancies between stimuli may influence vocalization changes to social situations as well. The patterns of fixation and vocalization to the cube and light sequences illustrate a progression from nonspecific responding at 5 ½ and 7 ½ months to inhibition of vocalization at 9 ½ months—and increased vocalization following moderately discrepant information at 11 ½ months, at least for female infants in our research. In the light sequence, females displayed increased vocalization only when the standard stimulus reappeared, following the moderate discrepancy trials. Males displayed increased vocalization only to the repetition of the standard light sequence, just as they did in the repetition trials of the cube sequence; hence, vocalizations for the boys seemed to announce boredom. Increased attention to a stimulus with age indicates that infants are generating ideas, whereas increased vocalization to slight discrepancies at 11½ months implies that the female infants vocalized to announce recognition—that is, the matching of an idea with a stimulus. In another study, this pattern of elicited vocalization to non-social stimuli by females was found to occur for infant males in response to social stimulation (Roe, 1975). Mothers were asked to encourage babbling, cooing, and other neutral vocalizations during a 3-minute session of verbal interaction at 3, 5, 7, 9, 11, 13, and 15 months of age in two longitudinal samples of 28 first-born boys. Roe reported that "vocal responsiveness of the subjects to stimulation was high at 3 and 5 months, decreased appreciably around 9 months, and increased again around 11 months of age" (p. 939). Roe's results are consistent with Lewis's (1959) suggestion that vocalization to adult speech increases at around 10 months of age prior to the onset of the first spoken words.

Increased vocalization, following the decrease at about nine months, may begin to serve an intentional communicative function. Infant vocalization appears to accompany cognitive excitement, which may set the stage for preverbal communication and the onset of the infant's first spoken words—an event that occurs at about 12 months (Bayley, 1969). This suggestion is bolstered by Bruner's (1975) observations that it is not until after 10 months of age that gesturing, pointing, and intonation accompany vocalization in conversational situations. Bruner and others (for example, Harding and Golinkoff, 1979) acknowledge that there are cognitive prerequisites for the onset of speech, although the nature of these prerequisites has not been specified.

The results from a study by Leung and Rheingold (1981) support the notion that infants use vocalization communicatively at around one year of age, but also indicate that other behaviors, such as pointing, often accompany communicative vocalizations. These authors sought to discover the age at which infants called interesting objects to another's attention. Four groups of infants—ages 10½, 12½, 14½ and 16½ months—were studied with their mothers in a setting that contained six stimulus objects likely to elicit attention-getting gestures. It was not until 12½ months of age that the majority of infants (nine of sixteen) pointed to these stimulus objects. In addition, pointing often accompanied vocalization and sometimes even looking at the mother. Eighty-seven percent of the infants' pointing acts (236 of 267) were accompanied by vocalizations.

The findings from these studies indicate that the increased vocalizations around 1 year of age are intentional and may be precursors to the onset of productive language. Holophrastic speech (speaking in one-word utterances, which often seem to carry meaning far beyond the single word) commences with the infant's ability to correctly label an object and implies that the infant has a mental image of the object. For spontaneous speech, a specific vocal utterance (for example, "ball"), must be associated with a particular stimulus for the stimulus to elicit the word. The infant also must be able to decode the acoustic elements within the speech stream, compare that information to an internalized model of a specific word, and articulate the phonological features necessary to produce a spoken word. It appears that the year-old child must have the capacity to activate specific thoughts and their auditory referents and to articulate the production of the remembered sound in order to label objects correctly. We can, therefore, hypothesize that the capacity to generate ideas may set the stage for this linguistic change.

Object Use

The use of the hypothetico-deductive method led to a specific prediction in a different domain of development. We reasoned that if vocalization and other behaviors in both social and nonsocial situations imply a capacity to generate specific ideas readily, then this ability should be observable in a different domain of development—that is, in the quality of a child's play. Specifically, the year-old infant should readily display functional uses for objects. Functional play would begin to occur reliably at 11½ but not 9½ months of age.

Zelazo and Kearsley (1980) examined a cross-sectional sample of sixty-four children during a fifteen-minute free-play sequence. There were eight infants of each sex at four ages—9½, 11½, 13½, and 15½ months. Six sets of toys that lent themselves to thirty-six unambiguous, appropriate uses were available to the children. In addition to the occurrence of functional play, operationally defined as the use of objects according to their adult-determined purposes, incidences of relational and stereotypical play were recorded. Relational play was defined as the use of two or more objects in an inappropriate or idiosyncratic way, whereas stereotypical play included mouthing, waving, banging, and fingering of objects. The results for the three measures at each of the four ages supported the prediction of a behavioral metamorphosis at about 1 year of age. Stereotypical play occurred most often at 9½ months (87 percent of total active play) and decreased sharply after that (only 22 percent of total active play by 15½ months). In contrast, functional play occurred the least at 9½ months and increased steadily with age to become the dominant activity by 15½ months (52 percent of total active play). Functional play did not become a statistically significant or reliably elicited phenomenon until 11½ months (16 percent of total active play). Of equal importance, the mean number of different appropriate uses for the toys also increased linearly from .32 to 2.62 to 7.88 to 10.38 over the four ages, not becoming a reliable phenomenon until 11½ months. In addition, the majority of children (twelve out of sixteen) did not both display functional play and reveal more than one functional act until 11½ months of age. By 13½ months, all children showed this pattern. Relational play increased and then decreased over this same period and appears to be a transitional behavior that bridges the development of play from stereotypical to functional use of objects.

These results reveal an increase in both the specificity and generality of object manipulations over this six-month period. The older the child is, the more likely that he or she will know both the behaviors specific to a particular toy and those appropriate to different toys. The increase in both diversity and specificity in functional play lends strong support to the hypothesis that the cognitive change that occurs around a year of age involves the capacity to generate specific ideas for specific situations. Also, these findings imply that the behavioral metamorphosis at one year involves changes in central processing ability, not neuromotor facility by itself. The neuromotor facility of the 9½-month-old infant is sufficient to perform many of the behaviors displayed by the older child. The primary change that occurs between 9½ and 11½ months is a qualitative one, which involves the child's knowledge of the conventional uses for these objects. The 9½-month-old infant is very likely to bang the receiver to the toy telephone, wave, and mouth it; the 11½-month-old child is more likely to put the receiver to his ear, babble, or even attempt to dial the phone.

Belsky and Most (1981) not only replicated the progression from stereotypical to functional play, but studied this progression's extension into symbolic pretend uses. Various types of play, increasing in degree of abstraction, were arranged in a Guttman Scale that showed a sequential progression for children between the ages of 7 and 21 months. In this procedure for studying developmental sequences, every child must display all tasks up to a given point and fail all tasks beyond that point. The point of change is indicative of the child's level of development in that particular domain and implies that children at a given optimal level do not display tasks that require a higher level of cognition.

Results from several recent studies of functional use of objects imply that practice is essential in order to establish an optimal level of performance. In one study, Zelazo and Kearsley (1981) observed that children with developmental delays (due to unknown causes) who did not have an opportunity for practice on a task functioned below their optimal level. Information-processing ability, measured by the use of sequences of visual and auditory stimuli (Zelazo, 1979, 1982a), was at a more sophisticated level than children's use of objects. However, specific efforts to promote functional and symbolic play, as in the case study reported by Zelazo and Kearsley (1980), resulted in a sharp improvement in the type of play over relatively brief time periods. In a related study by Parsons (1982), children with poor vision were compared with normally sighted children in a free play setting that included the same set of functional toys used by Zelazo and Kearsley. The total amount of functional play observed in children with poor vision was lower, although the number of different appropriate uses of objects, which imply basic cognitive ability, was similar to that of the normally sighted children. Parsons concludes that children with low vision have fewer opportunities to see and therefore use such toys less, even though they may be aware of their appropriate uses.

Both studies strongly implicate the role of practice for achieving an optimal level of development, as Fischer (1980) argues. These findings indicate that where opportunities for practice occur, there is a high interval synchrony between central-processing ability and the display of functional uses of objects. However, in situations where practice has been restricted, interval synchrony will not occur—and an optimal level for this performance of a behavior will not be reached.

Social Behavior

Each of the areas of research considered thus far—reactions to information processing, the communicative uses of vocalization and pointing in social situations, and quality of the child's object use, which includes the communicative nature of functional play—imply that the behavioral metamorphosis that takes place at 1 year of age should influence social development as well. The qualitative change in central-processing ability inferred from these studies indicates that relatively abrupt changes in social behavior should occur at about the same time. For example, reexamination of a sample of the research on fear of strangers reveals a greater consistency among studies than is usually acknowledged and greater similarity to protest on separation from the caregiver than previously supposed (Waters and others, 1975).

Stranger Fear. In a brief review of studies of stranger anxiety in which the data permitted reexamination of the criteria for "fear of strangers," Zelazo (1982b) makes an important distinction that has not been noted previously. If mild reactions, including a wrinkled brow or a wary avoidant gaze, are used as an indication of distress, an infant's fear of strangers first emerges at about 8 months of age. However, if less ambiguous, active measures of fear—including withdrawal, resistance, a "cry" face, or audible crying—are used as the criteria, stranger fear does not occur until about 12 months. He argues that data for social stimuli like those for nonsocial stimuli, imply that wariness and crying may be qualitatively different responses, reflecting different processes. Wariness may indicate quiet, attentive inhibition during information processing, which may culminate in any number of possible outcomes—including disinterest, crying, or smiling. If wariness culminates in uncertainty, distress may occur; if it culminates in assimilation, pleasure may occur. A less ambiguous, active reaction such as crying therefore has greater face validity as a measure of stranger anxiety than does wariness. With use of the strict criterion that a majority of children must show an active type of distress, fear of strangers does not occur as a reliable phenomenon until about 12 months of age—about the same age that children begin to gain the capacity for active thought.

Zelazo argues further that the situations used to elicit stranger fear and separation protest have greater similarity than previously believed. In most of the research on stranger fear, a crucial procedural step is employed to elicit distress successfully. Morgan and Ricciuti (1965) demonstrated that stranger fear could not be elicited readily unless the child was physically separated from his or her mother — usually by a distance of at least four feet. This procedural manipulation reveals that operationally there is little difference between the conditions necessary to elicit fear of strangers and separation protest.

Separation Protest. In one of the more extensive systematic investigations of separation distress, infant protests did not occur at a statistically significant level until 1 year of age (Kotelchuck and others, 1975). A series of carefully ordered sequences with mother, father, and stranger departures were presented to 144 infants (twelve boys and twelve girls at 6, 9, 12, 15, 18, and 21 months of age). Each child played in the middle of the room, equally distant from two seated adults. Unlike the stranger-fear procedure, the adults did not approach or pick up the infant; they simply departed according to a predetermined schedule after remaining in the room for three minutes. The principal dependent measures included crying, inhibiting of play, following the adult upon departure, and touching the adult upon reunion. The results for the four measures were inconsistent. None of the measures of protest occurred reliably in infants at 6 or 9 months of age, but the target behaviors all began to occur reliably at 12 months, intensified at 15 and 18 months, and declined at 21 months of age. In addition, the infants protested when left alone with only the stranger, but did not do so at their mother's departure if their fathers remained in the room or vice-versa. This finding indicates the similarity between separation protest and stranger fear.

How might the capacity for generating specific ideas produce these social phenomena? If the year-old infant is capable of active thought, then perhaps he is able to ask himself about the consequences of the stranger's approach or of an unfamiliar situation. The capacity to activate an idea in these settings implies that several outcomes to the situation are possible, and this uncertainty may result in an overt expression of fear. In effect, when a child cries he or she may be asking, "What is happening?"

In this situation as in the previous nonsocial domains, there appears to be high interval synchrony in the onset of these various behaviors at 1 year of age. However, the resolution of separation protest, in particular, may depend on appropriate experience and practice; this implies that interval synchrony for resolution may not occur. As children learn through experience that separation is regularly followed by reunion and that strange people become familiar with repeated exposure, their distress diminishes.

Implications for Theory and Practice

The capacity to generate ideas quickly is probably not a sufficient condition for the development of many new behaviors. The child also needs to have certain experiences through which he or she can learn to express this newly acquired central-processing capacity in conventional ways. For example, as illustrated clearly in a recent experiment, children with delays in speaking can develop productive language if they have appropriate linguistic models to imitate and if their caregivers show positive contingent responses following their attempts to speak (Zelazo and others, in press). Similarly, children need experiences with unfamiliar adults and places to resolve their uncertainty about strangers and strange settings. In still another domain, functional objects must be available and their uses demonstrated, even incidentally, if functional play is to result. Each new behavioral development may be dependent upon maturation of a common cognitive capacity, but the particular form of expression appears to be a learned phenomenon that is dependent upon a particular culture, family unit, and language.

There are at least two major implications that can be derived from this analysis. The first is a practical one: If children with developmental delays can be shown to have passed through the cognitive transition that occurs at about a year, the cause of their delays can then be identified as experiential in origin. Zelazo and Kearsley (1981) conducted an experimental longitudinal investigation to test this notion. In one portion of the study, a sample of 22-month-old children, who had mean delays of about 8 months as measured on the mental portion of the Bayley Scales, were sorted into intact and impaired information-processing groups using the light sequence and other stimuli. Children who assimilated the return portions of the sequences were defined as intact, whereas those who did not were considered impaired. Both groups were given ten months of intensive treatment to facilitate productive language and age-appropriate object use, including functional play. Behavior problems that interfered with the treatment, such as excessive crying and noncompliance, were eliminated as well. As predicted, children whose information-processing ability was intact overcame their delays in behavioral development through the treatment, whereas impaired children did not.

A second theoretical implication concerns the assumptions made about sensorimotor intelligence. We maintain that central-processing ability may create a readiness for a number of behavioral developments—a markedly different view from the traditional analysis in terms of sensorimotor intelligence. The detection of central-processing ability, possibly using the information-processing procedures, implies that mental and motor development, although usually thought to interact, may proceed independently. We argue that it may be necessary to expand the notion of sensorimotor intelligence to include more subtle motor expressions than the gross and fine motor indices that are usually measured (Zelazo, 1979, 1982a). This suggestion is consistent not only with the demonstration of memory formation and assimilation using the information-processing procedures described here, but also with the past twenty years of research on the determinants of attention studied by other investigators (for example, Cohen and Gelber, 1975; Fagan, 1978; Lewis, 1970; McCall and Kagan, 1967). Findings from such studies indicate that

48

although many normally developing children display synchrony between their information-processing capacities and their expressive behaviors, tests of mental ability that rely on expressive behaviors early in development (for example, Bayley, 1969; Griffiths, 1954) may be prone to error—particularly when used with handicapped infants. In fact, traditional tests of infant–toddler development are known to have poor predictive validity (Stott and Ball, 1965; Bayley, 1970). Direct measures of central-processing ability that rely less on experience and practice for the expression of such abilities are possible (Zelazo, 1979, 1982a). Perhaps the definition of sensorimotor intelligence should be modified to accommodate the evidence for information-processing ability.

Conclusion

Each of the social and nonsocial domains discussed in this chapter consistently reveals changes in behavior that imply a distinct transition in central-processing ability. The behavioral metamorphosis that occurs toward the end of the first year of life reflects a transformation from indiscriminate reactivity at about 7 ½ months to inhibition at 9 ½ months, followed by specific communicative expressiveness in several domains at 11 ½ months. As reported in the studies reviewed here, it is not until about 12 months that vocalization occurs specifically to slightly discrepant information in the Standard-Transformation-Return procedure, vocalization and pointing occur reliably in social situations, and clear, active expressions of fear occur in stranger-fear and separation-protest experimental situations. However, the emergence of functional play at 11 ½ months of age gives the clearest indication of the nature of the cognitive metamorphosis that may dictate these changes. We hypothesize that each of these varied developments can be accounted for by a specific change in central-processing capacity—namely, the capacity to generate specific associations readily. This ability, similar to a popular notion of the capacity to generate an idea, accounts for the increase in both specificity and diversity of behavior at 1 year of age, which is not explained easily by maturation of neuromotor ability or learning alone. One theoretical implication is that the traditional view of sensorimotor intelligence may need to be modified. One practical implication is that evidence of the capacity to generate ideas may permit the identification of normal intelligence among some developmentally delayed children.

References

Bayley, N. *Bayley Scales of Infant Development*. New York: Psychological Corporation, 1969.
Bayley, N. "Development of Mental Abilities." In P. H. Mussen (Ed.), *Carmichael's Manual of Child Psychology*. Vol. 1. New York: Wiley, 1970.
Belsky, J., and Most, R. "From Exploration to Play: A Cross-sectional Study of Infant Free Play Behavior." *Developmental Psychology*, 1981, *17*, 630–639.
Bruner, J. S. "The Ontogenesis of Speech Acts." *Journal of Child Language*, 1975, *2*, 1–19.

Cohen, L. B., and Gelber, E. R. "Infant Visual Memory." In L. Cohen and P. Salapatek (Eds.), *Infant Perception: From Sensation to Cognition: Basic Visual Process.* New York: Academic Press, 1975.

Fagan, J. F. "Infant Recognition Memory and Early Cognitive Ability: Empirical, Theoretical, and Remedial Considerations." In F. D. Minifie and L. L. Lloyd (Eds.), *Communicative and Cognitive Abilities: Early Behavioral Assessment.* Baltimore: University Park Press, 1978.

Fischer, K. W. "A Theory of Cognitive Development: The Control and Construction of Hierarchies of Skills." *Psychological Review,* 1980, *87,* 477–531.

Fischer, K. W., and Bullock, D. "Patterns of Data: Sequence, Synchrony, and Constraint in Cognitive Development." In K. W. Fischer (Ed.), *Cognitive Development.* New Directions for Child Development, no. 12. San Francisco: Jossey-Bass, 1981.

Griffiths, R. *The Abilities of Babies.* London: University of London, 1954.

Harding, G. G., and Golinkoff, R. M. "The Origins of Intentional Vocalizations in Prelinguistic Infants." *Child Development,* 1979, *50,* 33–40.

Kagan, J. "Do Infants Think?" *Scientific American,* 1972, *226,* 74–82.

Kagan, J., Kearsley, R. B., and Zelazo, P. R. *Infancy: Its Place in Human Development.* Cambridge, Mass.: Harvard University Press, 1978.

Kahneman, D., Tursky, B., Shapiro, D., and Crider, A. "Pupillary Heart Rate and Skin Resistance Changes During a Mental Task." *Journal of Experimental Psychology,* 1969, *79,* 164–167.

Kotelchuck, M., Zelazo, P. R., Kagan, J., and Spelke, E. "Infant Reactions to Parental Separations When Left with Familiar and Unfamiliar Adults." *Journal of Genetic Psychology,* 1975, *126,* 225–262.

Leung, E. H., and Rheingold, H. "The Development of Pointing as a Social Gesture." *Developmental Psychology,* 1981, *17,* 215–220.

Lewis, M. M. *How Children Learn to Speak.* New York: Basic Books, 1959.

Lewis, M. "Individual Differences in the Measurement of Early Cognitive Growth." In J. Hellmuth (Ed.), *Exceptional Infant.* Vol. 2. New York: Brunner/Mazel, 1970.

McCall, R. B., Eichorn, D. H., and Hogarty, P. S. "Transitions in Early Mental Development," *Monographs of the Society for Research in Child Development,* 1977, *42,* entire issue.

McCall, R. B., and Kagan, J. "Stimulus-Schema Discrepancy and Attention in the Infant." *Journal of Experimental Child Psychology,* 1967, *5,* 381–390.

Morgan, G. A., and Ricciuti, H. N. "Infants' Responses to Strangers During the First Year." In B. M. Foss (Ed.), *Determinants of Infant Behavior. IV.* London: Methuen, 1965.

Parsons, A. S. "An Exploratory Study on the Patterns of Emerging Play Behavior in Young Children with Low Vision." Unpublished doctoral dissertation, University of Texas at Austin, 1982.

Roe, K. V. "Amount of Infant Vocalization as a Function of Age: Some Cognitive Implications." *Child Development,* 1975, *46,* 936–941.

Stott, L. H., and Ball, R. S. "Infant and Preschool Mental Tests: Review and Evaluation." *Monographs of the Society for Research in Child Development,* 1965, *30,* entire issue.

Waters, E., Matas, L., and Sroufe, L. A. "Infants' Reactions to an Approaching Stranger: Description, Validation, and Functional Significance of Wariness." *Child Development,* 1975, *46,* 348–356.

Zelazo, P. R. "Reactivity to Perceptual-Cognitive Events: Application for Infant Assessment." In R. B. Kearsley and I. Sigel (Eds.), *Infants at Risk: The Assessment of Cognitive Functioning.* Hillsdale, N.J.: Erlbaum, 1979.

Zelazo, P. R. "An Alternative Assessment Procedure for Handicapped Infants and Toddlers: Theoretical and Practical Issues." In D. Bricker (Ed.), *Application of*

50

Research Findings to Intervention with At-Risk Handicapped Infants. Baltimore: University Park Press, 1982a.

Zelazo, P. R. "The Year-Old Infant: A Period of Major Cognitive Change." In T. Bever (Ed.), *Regressions in Development: Basic Phenomena and Theories.* Hillsdale, N.J.: Erlbaum, 1982b.

Zelazo, P. R., Kagan, J., and Hartmann, R. "Excitement and Boredom as Determinants of Vocalization in Infants." *Journal of Genetic Psychology,* 1975, *126,* 107–117.

Zelazo, P. R., and Kearsley, R. B. "The Emergence of Functional Play in Infants: Evidence for a Major Cognitive Transition." *Journal of Applied Developmental Psychology,* 1980, *1,* 95–117.

Zelazo, P. R., and Kearsley, R. B. "Cognitive Assessment and Intervention for Developmentally Delayed Infants." *Educational Resources Information Center.* Final Report to the Office of Special Education (Grant #G007603979), 1981.

Zelazo, P. R., Kearsley, R. B., and Ungerer, J. *Learning to Speak: A Manual for Parents.* Hillsdale, N.J.: Erlbaum, in press.

Philip R. Zelazo is director of the Center for Infant-Toddler Development, St. Elizabeth's Hospital, Brighton, Massachusetts, and associate professor, Tufts University School of Medicine. His research interests include the development of cognitive, social, and motor abilities in early childhood and the creation of alternative tests of development.

Elizabeth L. Leonard is a candidate for a Ph.D. in psychology at Tufts University. Her research interests are in infant perception and cognition.

Representational skills seem to emerge in a stagelike fashion
at approximately 2 years of age.

The Development of
Representational Skills

Roberta Corrigan

Attempts to address whether human cognitive abilities develop in a stagelike
fashion have occupied countless pages in the developmental literature. But
most researchers maintain that, to demonstrate the existence of stages in cognitive development, clear developmental sequences within task domains must
first be established (Siegler, 1981). Then, synchronous patterns of change
must be shown across domains, suggesting the presence of across-the-board
stages (Flavell, 1982).

The present chapter examines the possible stagelike development of representational skills. A definition of *mental representation* will be discussed first. Then
examples of cognitive tasks that seem to require simple representational skills will
be reviewed, and evidence from the developmental literature on relationships
among these tasks will be examined. Finally, new data will be presented showing qualitative changes that occur roughly at the same time across selected representational skills at around 2 years of age—thus suggesting the existence of cognitive stages. The traditional explanation for cognitive stages is that general underlying structures control many different types of cognitive functioning (Piaget,
1971), but the data reviewed in this chapter fit better within a framework such
as the one described by Fischer and Pipp (forthcoming). They describe a developmental model in which stagelike development occurs because of changes in the
upper limits (the optimal level) of the complexity of skills that children can control.

K. W. Fischer (Ed.). *Levels and Transitions in Children's Development.* New Directions
for Child Development, no. 21. San Francisco: Jossey-Bass, September 1983.

Defining Mental Representation

The question of continuity versus discontinuity in development is com-plicated, especially in the case of constructs like *representation*, where there is no general consensus among researchers on how to define or measure it (Corri-gan, 1979). Piaget ([1946] 1951), defined representation as the ability to use symbols in order to make absent objects, people, and events present. He argued that all symbolic capacities—including deferred imitation, pretend play, language, mental images, and recall memory—require mental represen-tation. Other developmental theorists also equate symbolic thinking with representation (for example, Bates, 1979; Curtiss and others, 1981; McCune-Nicolich, 1981). However, cognitive psychologists, who primarily study infor-mation processing, learning, problem solving, and memory in adults, use the term *representation* to describe the ways that knowledge may be coded, organiz-ed, and stored in the brain (as in images, propositional networks, schemas, and so on). Similarly, many developmental psychologists use representation as a synonym for the construction, retrieval, and recall of information (Kagan, 1979) and argue that representation and symbolic development are not equivalent (Wolf and Gardner, 1981).

In the present chapter, the term *representation* is not limited to either symbolic or memory abilities, because a child is capable of different kinds of memory and symbolic skills depending upon his or her level of development (Corrigan, 1979). Instead, the term is used to designate one level in the devel-opment of cognitive skills. According to Fischer's (1980) skill theory, children's cognitive abilities develop through a hierarchy of levels. In infancy, children use increasingly complex sensory and motor skills to act on objects, eventually constructing what are called systems of sensorimotor actions at about 1 year of age. Representation as a mental structure results when two such systems of sensorimotor actions are combined by the child. With the onset of represen-tation, children understand that objects, events, and people have properties that are independent of the children's own actions. They also perceive that objects can be used in many different complex sensorimotor activities and that objects can produce many different types of actions. For example, an infant may have one sensorimotor system that allows her to understand that when she pushes a ball on the floor, it rolls. She may also note that after she sees someone else push the ball, it rolls. When these two sensorimotor systems are joined to form a simple representation, she comes to realize that one character-istic of a ball is that it rolls.

According to skill theory, representational skills continue to develop in complexity as they are combined with each other into higher-level skills (Fischer, 1980). These more complex levels of representation are beyond the scope of this chapter, which focuses on the initial acquisition of represen-tation.

Examples of Representational Skills

There seem to be a number of cognitive tasks that potentially require simple representational skills for their solution, including tasks involving object permanence, seriation, pretend play, and language.

Object Permanence. According to Piaget's stage theory ([1937], 1954), when children at Stage 6 of the sensorimotor period search for an object that is hidden in a container and then moved (while hidden) under a series of screens, they internally represent the path of the object and retrieve it by mentally retracing back through the order of hiding. This stage 6 object-permanence task, often called the invisible-displacements task, is the most frequently used measure of representation. However, the exact object-permanence task that is administered and the criteria applied in judging that the child has succeeded on the task vary widely among researchers (Corrigan, 1979). In fact, the usual solution of a typical invisible-displacements task probably requires sensorimotor rather than representational skills (Bertenthal and Fischer, 1983; Corrigan, 1981). That is, the child does not have to remember the object's path, but can solve the problem through use of trial-and-error search behaviors, persistent search, consistent search for the object in the same position, or use of other simple search strategies.

Nevertheless, invisible-displacements tasks can be useful indices of mental representation. For example, Fischer and Jennings (1981) and Bertenthal and Fischer (1983) argue that beginning at around 24 months, children attempt to shape their own search to match hiding strategies they detect in the experimenter. In other words, children mentally represent or map out the simple hiding strategies of the examiner, although they cannot yet represent the entire path of an invisibly displaced object. This ability to understand that another person can act independently of the child's own actions requires simple representational skills.

Application of stringent criteria to decide when children have passed invisible-displacements tasks reduces the likelihood that the children will succeed by pursuing only sensorimotor search strategies. For example, Corrigan (1981) showed one group of children objects hidden in a procedure similar to the traditional one used by Uzgiris and Hunt (1975), while she showed a second group of children objects hidden with a different procedure: In the latter procedure, the direction of hiding was alternated on each trial throughout a series of trials. Children in the first group were successful in their search more often than children in the alternating-trials group. Thus, the alternating-trials method of presentation appears to have required more sophisticated search strategies.

Seriation. Arranging a group of objects into an ordinal series has been described as a concrete operational ability. Although parallels to such operational seriation begin in infancy (Inhelder and Piaget, 1964), there have been only a few studies of sensorimotor seriation. Greenfield and others (1972) noted a sequence of nesting-cup seriation strategies in 11- to 36-month-olds. By 28 to 32 months, children were capable of seriating a five-cup structure but were unable to insert a sixth cup int the structure. Only the 36-month-olds were able to insert the sixth cup. A child must relate size in two directions when inserting a cup—that is, he or she must realize that the sixth cup is smaller than the cup on one side of it and larger than the cup on the other side. That is, the child combines two sensorimotor systems, one for putting little cups into big cups with another for taking smaller cups out of larger ones. In doing this, the child comes to view size as an independent attribute of the cups. Thus, seriation of nesting cups that involves inserting another element appears to require simple representational skills.

Language. Language ability encompasses a wide variety of different cognitive skills. Deciding which skills are to be included under the umbrella term *language* and which of those skills require representation are two different theoretical issues of relevance to the discussion here.

Should skills such as inferring other's intentions and taking turns in conversations be considered linguistic or extralinguistic? That is, are communicative rules and grammatical rules separate entities? Researchers like Curtiss and others (1981) maintain that early nongrammatical language may be pragmatically and conceptually based but argue that later grammatical language requires separate, purely linguistic, rule systems. A somewhat different position is taken by Fischer and Corrigan (1981), who argue that different language skills will develop independently and unevenly in the same child. The social-communicative, referential, and grammatical language components proposed by Curtiss and others can be viewed as consisting of separate skills that may or may not be related to one another. They may be linked to other language skills or to other nonlanguage, cognitive skills at different points in development.

Fischer and Corrigan also predict that the first words and the first two-word combinations (for example, those acquired through imitation or as unanalyzed units) are usually not representational because they do not require the use of coordinated multiple sensorimotor systems. Only later in development are sensorimotor systems combined into simple representations: This allows for more efficient vocabulary learning—which leads to a vocabulary spurt—and the learning of specific production rules for semantic relations in two-word utterances—which result in a spurt in two-word productions.

Pretend Play. Certain types of pretend play require simple representational skills. Children must view their habitual actions upon objects as separate from the objects themselves during pretend play, which allows the children to use the objects in new ways. For example, Watson and Fischer (1977) argue that the use of substitute objects as representatives of something else requires the child to differentiate the original object from its action and to associate the action with a new object. Similarly, Corrigan (1982) states that pretend play involves a sequence of skills requiring increasing control over a number of variables, which include both the number of animate and inanimate components expressed in the play episode and the number of symbolic substitutions (use of one object to stand for another) that the child produces.

Spurts and Plateaus Across Diverse Representational Skills

This section of the chapter reviews the literature for evidence that the representational skills discussed previously show changes at approximately the same time in development. Evidence for such stagelike emergence of representational skills comes from two different sources: (1) studies that attempt to define major developmental transition points involving a large variety of cognitive skills and (2) studies that examine more limited synchronies across a few skill areas.

Recent findings from divergent sources (McCall, 1979; Kagan, 1979) suggest that there may be several general periods of discontinuity in infancy at approximately 2-to-3, 8, 13, and 21 months of age. Both the 13- and 21-month transition points have been identified as the time when representational activities first begin. For example, Nelson (1979) and Bowerman (1978) suggest that the most important Stage 6 representational developments occur prior to 14 months of age, which indicates that the child's sensorimotor development is finished by the beginning of the second year. On the other hand, McCall (1979) describes the 21-month transition point as the time when children become capable of drawing "symbolic relationships between entities."

Instead of looking at general periods of discontinuity, many other studies have focused on specific relationships between skills. For example, several researchers have reported general correlations between pretend play and language during the age period of 12-to-36 months (Bates, 1979; McCune-Nicolich and Bruskin, forthcoming). Wolf and Gardner (1981) analyze the relationship between language and pretend play in longitudinal data taken from four children. They found major transitions at 13 and 20 months in role-structuring — the ability to understand the function of various objects and people in relation to a central action. At 13 months the children began to use props as recipients of actions in play and to use single words in speech. At 20 months the children began to use the props in an agent role (carrying out actions) rather than a recipient role (receiving actions), and they started to use two-word utterances in speech. In addition, Corrigan (1982) examines the development of play and language skills following the 20-month transition point. Only children at the most advanced pretend play levels (involving symbolic substitutions of both the play agent and object) produced non-prototypical language using either inanimate subjects or animate objects.

The relationship between object permanence and language has also been the focus of much research (see Corrigan, 1979, for a comprehensive review). Results of the research are contradictory, depending upon the type of object-permanence task used and the language measure employed. In general, few studies have reported major correlations between language and object permanence, although some specific relationships have been reported.

Watson and Fischer (1977) investigated the relationship between object permanence and pretend play. Only 19 percent of their thirty-six infants showed synchrony between play and object-permanence level. Seven infants displayed play behaviors that were more advanced than the predicted object-permanence level, and ten infants showed the reverse pattern. As discussed previously, many of the infants scoring at the highest object-permanence level probably did so by using sensorimotor skills (such as trial-and-error search behavior) rather than the simple representational skills necessary to produce the most complex pretend play activities. While this and other studies reported in this section suggest some specific relationships between various representational skills, they are far from conclusive in consistently showing stagelike emergence of those skills. New data are available, however, that test directly for the occurrence of approximately simultaneous spurts and plateaus across diverse representational skills.

New Evidence for Stagelike Emergence of Representational Skills

The data to be discussed in this section come from a longitudinal study of language and cognitive development and a cross-sectional study of language, object permanence, and seriation. Some portions of the data have been reported elsewhere (Corrigan, 1978, 1982), and some are reported here for the first time. The longitudinal data were collected from three children—John, Mindy, and Ashley—during an 18-month period from 1974 through 1976. The children, who were 9, 10, and 11 months of age at the beginning of the study, were videotaped in a free-play situation every third week in their homes and audiotaped during intervening weeks. The children in the cross-sectional study ranged in age from 10 to 26 months. Six children at each of 10, 14, 18, 22, and 26 months were videotaped in the laboratory while involved in free play and attempting the same cognitive tasks used in the longitudinal study.

Cognitive Tasks: Object Permanence, Seriation, Pretend Play, and Language. A modified version of the Uzgiris and Hunt (1975) scale was administered to children in both studies to test for object-permanence development. The modifications produced a twenty-one-step scale (see Corrigan, 1978, for a detailed description) that included several systematic variations in the hiding procedure: hiding the objects under one, two, and three screens; hiding them from right to left and from left to right; and using visible and invisible displacements of the objects. The highest steps of the scale involved the systematic search task, which required that the children retrace the path of the object in the reverse of the order in which it was hidden. Each child was assigned a score based on the highest step attained in any session.

Seriation ability was tested in both the longitudinal and cross-sectional studies by asking children to nest five cups, one inside the other. Following Greenfield and others (1972), the cups were first arranged in front of the children for up to four trials in one of two orders. In cases where children produced a five-cup structure, they were told to "put this one where it belongs." Children were given a score for the most complex seriated structure they produced on any trial (two, three, four, five cups, or five cups with insertion of the sixth).

During the free play portion of the longitudinal study, the children often engaged in make-believe play, although no attempt was made to specifically elicit such behaviors. Instances of pretend play were categorized according to the number of symbolic substitutions (use of one object to stand for another) of either an agent or object used in the play sequences. For example, if the children pretended that a doll was talking on a telephone that was represented by a seashell, they were scored as having produced two symbolic substitutions.

The cross-sectional study employed only general language measures because the children were seen only once for a brief time period. Measures of length of utterance have been shown to be useful indicators of children's general linguistic level. The children's most advanced language performance (their greatest length of utterance) was used, rather than their mean utterance length, in order to make the language measures consistent with other cognitive tasks—which also measured the children's most advanced performances. The longitudinal study employed language measures that required more extensive data samples in addition to measures of utterance length. The total number of vocabulary items was tracked over time for each child. And the number and type of animate and inanimate components in each production also was scored in order to provide a language measure parallel to the pretend play measure. (See Corrigan, 1982, for more details of the language scoring.)

Results and Discussion. Table 1 shows the ages when various representational skills were first produced by the three children in the longitudinal study. Between 11 and 14 months of age, all three children began to retrieve objects that were invisibly hidden. This was followed by a long plateau period, in which the children used sensorimotor search strategies to retrieve an object when it was invisibly displaced, but did so inconsistently—sometimes searching under other screens before finding the object under the end screen, or finding the object when it was hidden in one direction but not the other. Finally, between 18 and 21 months of age, the children began to systematically retrieve the object, regardless of how it was hidden. As discussed earlier, this type of behavior may have required the use of simple representational skills.

In the seriation task, the children began to make seriation attempts between 11 and 13 months. This was followed by a long plateau period, in which only quantitative changes occurred—that is, changes in the number of cups seriated and in the children's persistence in their seriation attempts. Then at 18 to 21 months of age, another qualitative reorganization occurred when

Table 1. Age of First Production of Representational Skills

Type of Representational Skill	Age of First Production		
	John	Mindy	Ashley
Object Permanence			
visible hiding		10.0 *	10.13*
invisible hiding	12.6 *	10.28	11.6
invisible displacement (partial)	13.23	12.24	11.6
invisible displacement (complete)	20.16	18.0	16.14
systematic search	20.16	18.23	18.11
Seriation			
zero cups	12.6 *	10.0 *	10.13*
two cups	12.22	12.24	11.6
three, four, five cups	15.25	14.14	13.16
five cups with insertion cup	21.6	19.19	18.11
Pretend Play			
no pretending	12.6 *	10.0 *	10.13*
zero substitutions	15.5	12.24	12.3
one substitution	24.13	22.20	23.22
two substitutions	27.25		
Language Components			
none		10.0 *	10.13*
one inanimate	12.6 *	14.14	14.26
one animate	13.23	14.25	17.25
animate + inanimate	20.16	24.26	20.14
non-prototypical	23.22	26.28	26.2

* Age at first testing
Note: Age is recorded in months and days.

the children began to insert a sixth cup into a five-cup seriated structure. At this time, this skill was not consistently attained, since the children sometimes produced only lower-level seriation structures in subsequent testing. Thus, the full attainment of stable representational skills in seriation probably occurred later in these children than indicated by Table 1.

In their make-believe, the children first began at 12 to 15 months to use pre-symbolic play with no symbolic substitutions—that is, pretend activity that involved either themselves or passive others as the focus of their play, instead of active others or substitute objects. Once again, a long plateau period followed, during which the children extended the same activities to a wider variety of actions and objects. Finally, at 23 to 24 months of age, they began using substitute objects and agents in their spontaneous pretend activities.

All the children used language that expressed one inanimate or animate component by 14 months, which paralleled the use of presymbolic play involving either themselves or passive others. Between 21 and 24 months of age, they began to express both animate and inanimate components in single

Figure 1. Spurts and Plateaus in New Vocabulary and Utterance Length

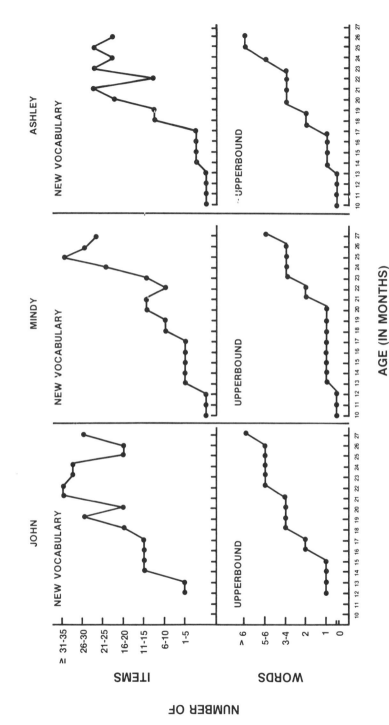

utterances and between 24 and 27 months they began to produce nonprototyp-
ical sentences — for example, those with an animate recipient or an inanimate
agent. Several other spurts and plateaus were also evident in the children's
developing language ability, as shown in Figure 1. At around 13 months, the
two girls began to produce single words during the observational sessions.
John used single words from the first testing session. Corrigan (1978) reports a
spurt in the total number of vocabulary items produced during each observational session at around 18 to 21 months of age. Another spurt is evident
between 18 and 21 months in Figure 1, with the largest number of *new* vocabulary items produced at 21 months for two of the children and at 26 months for
the third child. In addition, the spurt in new vocabulary occurred at roughly
the same time as the onset of multiword utterances by the two girls and the use
of much longer utterances by John. John apparently used a language acquisition strategy that was different from that of the two girls, making more use of
partial imitation of adult utterances, which allowed his language abilities
to develop at a faster rate (Corrigan, 1978).

The results from the cross-sectional study are remarkably similar to
those reported for the longitudinal one. The mean proportions of children
attaining the various cognitive skills tested are shown in Figure 2. On the
object-permanence task, there was a change in behavior between 10 and 14
months from searching for visibly displaced objects to searching for objects
that were invisibly hidden. The children in the cross-sectional study were not
given the extensive opportunity to practice and learn various search strategies
that those in the longitudinal study experienced, which is probably why little
change was evident in the attainment of object-permanence skills after 14
months. The only exception to this is a slight increase in attainment of the
highest object-permanence levels ("systematic"), beginning at 18 months. On
the seriation tasks, the cross-sectional children began to seriate two or more
cups between 10 and 14 months. At 26 months there was an additional spurt
when five of the six children first began to use the simple representational skills
necessary to insert a sixth cup into the seriated structure.

The first changes in language development occurred between 10 and
14 months of age. At 10 months, only one of the six children produced single-
word utterances, but, by 14 months, most of them (five out of six) were using
single words. At 18 months of age, none of the children produced multiword
utterances, but by 22 months, three of them had used such word combinations. The children's most advanced language performance, not shown in
Figure 2, spurted at 18 to 22 months, from a mean of 1.0 to 2.3 words per
utterance, as did the mean number of single words produced during the observational session — from a mean of 7.0 to 37.0 words. Figure 2 depicts another
spurt, at 22 to 26 months, when five of the six children produced multiword
utterances; the most advanced performance at 26 months also increased to a
mean of 3.9 words.

Although the two studies show some consistent behavioral changes, the

Figure 2. Proportion of Cross-Sectional Children Demonstrating
Highest Level of Object Permanence, Seriation, and Language Behaviors

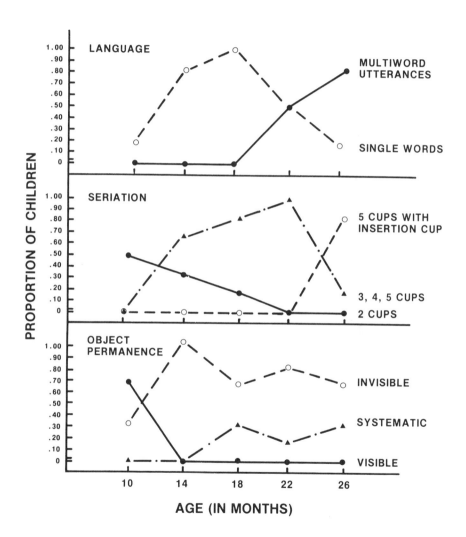

picture that emerges is not one of a rigid sequence of individual developments across domains. For example, amount of practice of the tasks seems to produce important differences between the longitudinal and cross-sectional data. In addition, in the longitudinal data, object permanence, seriation, and pretend-play variables were more advanced in the two girls, while the language variables were more advanced for John. Therefore, there was variation in the order of attainment and onset of different skills for different children. Also, most of the analyses presented here were somewhat global. Little attempt was made to delineate rules for task performance as Siegler (1981) has done or to make detailed task analyses like those of Fischer (1980). Such specific analyses should be undertaken in order to study more precisely why the cognitive domains overlapped where they did—and to predict whether there might be other overlaps in domains during the plateau periods because specific skills are shared.

Conclusion

It appears that representational skills do show stagelike behavior during early development: They show roughly synchronous patterns of change across skill domains. In the data presented in this chapter, major changes were evident at approximately 12-to-14 months and again at 18-to-21 months of age. These correspond to the general periods of discontinuity identified in other research (for example, McCall, 1979; Kagan, 1979). However, these "stages" bear only a superficial resemblance to Piaget's all-or-none, universal stages, which are hypothetically governed by single underlying structures. Instead, the stages discussed here are subject to environmental influences and to individual differences in rate and order of attainment. Therefore, they more closely resemble the looser stage notion described by Fischer and Pipp (forthcoming), which predicts changing upper limits in the complexity of skills a person can control. These changes cause periods of rapid development as the upper limit shifts, followed by plateau periods of growth when quantitative changes within skill domains occur.

References

Bates, E. (Ed.) *The Emergence of Symbols: Cognition and Communication in Infancy.* New York: Academic Press, 1979.

Bertenthal, B., and Fischer, K. W. "The Development of Representation in Search." *Child Development,* 1983, *54,* 846–857.

Bowerman, M. "Words and Sentences: Uniformity, Individual Variation, and Shifts over Time in Patterns of Acquisition." In F. Minifie and L. Lloyd (Eds.), *Communicative and Cognitive Abilities — Early Behavioral Assessment.* Baltimore, Md.: University Park Press, 1978.

Corrigan, R. "Language Development as Related to Stage 6 Object Permanence Development." *Journal of Child Language,* 1978, *5,* 173–189.

Corrigan, R. "Cognitive Correlates of Language: Differential Criteria Yield Differential Results." *Child Development,* 1979, *50,* 617–631.

Corrigan, R. "The Effects of Task and Practice on Search for Invisibly Displaced Objects." *Developmental Review,* 1981, *1,* 1–17.

Corrigan, R. "The Control of Animate and Inanimate Components in Pretend Play and Language." *Child Development,* 1982, *53,* 1343–1353.

Curtiss, S., Kempler, O., and Yamada, J. "The Relationship Between Language and Cognition in Development: Theoretical Framework and Research Design." U.C.L.A. *Working Papers in Cognitive Linguistics,* 1981, *3,* 1–60.

Fischer, K. W. "A Theory of Cognitive Development: The Control and Construction of Hierarchies of Skills." *Psychological Review,* 1980, *87,* 477–531.

Fischer, K. W., and Corrigan, R. "A Skill Approach to Language Development." In R. Stark (Ed.), *Language Behavior in Infancy and Early Childhood.* Amsterdam: Elsevier, 1981.

Fischer, K. W., and Jennings, S. "The Emergence of Representation in Search: Understanding the Hider as an Independent Agent." *Developmental Review,* 1981, *1,* 18–30.

Fischer, K. W., and Pipp, S. "Processes of Cognitive Development: Optimal Level and Skill Acquisition." In R. Sternberg (Ed.), *Mechanisms of Cognitive Development.* San Francisco: Freeman, forthcoming.

Flavell, J. "On Cognitive Development." *Child Development,* 1982, *53,* 1–10.

Greenfield, P., Nelson, K., and Saltzman, E. "The Development of Rule-Bound Strategies for Manipulating Seriated Cups: A Parellel Between Action and Grammer." *Cognitive Psychology,* 1972, *3,* 291–310.

Inhelder, R., and Piaget, J. *The Early Growth of Logic: Classification and Seriation.* London: Routledge & Kegan Paul, 1964.

Kagan, J. "Structure and Process in the Human Infant: The Ontogeny of Mental Representation." In M. Bornstein and W. Kessen (Eds.), *Psychological Development from Infancy: Image to Intention.* Hillsdale, N.J.: Erlbaum, 1979.

McCall, R. "The Development of Intellectual Functioning in Infancy and the Prediction of Later IQ." In J. Osofsky (Ed.), *Handbook of Infant Development.* New York: Wiley, 1979.

McCune-Nicolich, L. "Toward Symbolic Functioning: Structure of Early Pretence Games and Potential Parallels with Language." *Child Development,* 1981, *52,* 785–797.

McCune-Nicolich, L., and Bruskin, C. "Combinatorial Competency in Symbolic Play and Language." In P. Pepler and K. Rubin (Eds.), *The Play of Children: Current Theory and Research.* Basel, Switzerland: Karger, forthcoming.

Nelson, K. "The Role of Language in Infant Development." In M. Bornstein and W. Kessen (Eds.), *Psychological Development from Infancy: Image to Intention.* Hillsdale, N.J.: Erlbaum, 1979.

Piaget, J. *Play, Dreams, and Imitation in Childhood.* (C. Gattegno and F. M. Hodgson, trans.) New York: Norton, 1951. (Originally published 1946.)

Piaget, J. *The Construction of Reality in the Child.* (M. Cook, trans.) New York: Basic Books, 1954. (Originally published 1937.)

Piaget, J. "The Theory of Stages in Cognitive Development." In D. Green, M. Ford, and G. Flamer (Eds.), *Measurement and Piaget.* New York: McGraw-Hill, 1971.

Siegler, R. "Developmental Sequences Within and Between Concepts." *Monographs of the Society for Research in Child Development,* 1981, *46,* entire issue.

Uzgiris, I., and Hunt, J. *Assessment in Infancy: Ordinal Scales of Psychological Development.* Urbana: University of Illinois Press, 1975.

Watson, M., and Fischer, K. W. "A Developmental Sequence of Agent Use in Late Infancy." *Child Development,* 1977, *48,* 828–835.

Wolf, D., and Gardner, H. "On the Structure of Early Symbolization." In R. Schiefelbusch and D. Bricker (Eds.), *Early Language: Acquisition and Intervention.* Baltimore, Md.: University Park Press, 1981.

64

Roberta Corrigan is associate professor of educational psychology at the University of Wisconsin at Milwaukee. Her research focuses on language and cognitive development in late infancy and early childhood.

Major cognitive-developmental transitions seem to occur at approximately 2-to-4, 7-to-8, 13-to-14, and 18-to-21 months of age.

Exploring Developmental Transitions in Mental Performance

Robert B. McCall

The word *development* means *change* and developmental psychology is the study of behavioral changes within individuals at different ages (Wohlwill, 1973). One would expect that developmental psychologists spend much of their time charting behavioral growth as a function of age, describing major changes in behavioral dispositions over the life span, and identifying factors that influence quantitative and qualitative changes over developmental time periods in the behavior of species or individuals. But that is not what developmental psychologists typically do (McCall, 1977). We usually do not conduct longitudinal studies and even when we do, most of them are very short-term, consist of assessments at only two or three ages, and are not aimed at discovering changes but at detecting consistencies across age. For example, if you give many developmental psychologists a set of longitudinal data, they will immediately calculate cross-age correlations that reveal consistencies in individual differences across age, not change. Indeed, failure to find cross-age correlations is typically a disappointment to researchers, and the fact that major concepts (for example, intelligence and aggressiveness) cannot be defined or measured identically from one age to the next is a major methodological problem for most developmentalists.

K. W. Fischer (Ed.). *Levels and Transitions in Children's Development.* New Directions for Child Development, no. 21. San Francisco: Jossey-Bass, September 1983.

In short, developmental psychologists tend to regard changes in behavior as something to be avoided or overcome in research designs rather than something to be celebrated and studied. In a sense, we repudiate our *raison d'etre*. We are basically age-period psychologists, not developmentalists, and as a result we have failed to understand comprehensively the phenomena that we study (McCall, 1977, 1981). I will present two examples of this point here, but first some background information on the nature of change is required.

Developmental change may occur within two realms. The first is the *developmental function* (Wohlwill, 1973), which is essentially the average performance of a group on a single variable measured repeatedly over age. If height in inches were plotted across age for a random sample of humans, this graph would constitute a species-general developmental function for height in inches. Of course, such developmental functions may be plotted for males and females separately, for different races, or for any other categorization of subjects. Developmental functions are also either *continuous* or *discontinuous*. They are continuous if the same qualitative variable is measured at each age; this is the case for height in inches or vocabulary size. They are discontinuous if the qualitative nature of what is being measured changes from one age to the next, such as in Piagetian stages of sensorimotor development in the first two years.

Second, developmental change may occur within the realm of *individual differences* — that is, the degree of consistency in the relative rank ordering of subjects on a given variable from one age to another. Typically, developmentalists measure the degree of stability with a correlation coefficient. High correlations reflect stability in individual differences in performance across age, while low correlations reflect instability in the relative rank ordering of individuals across age. Unfortunately, instability — that is, change — is rarely tested directly. Instead, developmental researchers conclude that behavioral change has occurred when evidence for stability is not present, an inference that is logically unsound at best and illegitimate at worst.

In any case, developmental change can occur within the context of a developmental function independent of change across age in the individual differences in performance for a given variable. For example, just as the correlation between two sets of measurements is independent of the means of those two distributions (if they are symmetric), continuity and discontinuity in a developmental function are also potentially independent of stability and instability in individual differences. This means that evidence for stability does not necessarily imply continuity, and evidence for continuity does not necessarily imply stability. Our failure to understand developmental phenomena comprehensively occurs because we sometimes make generalizations from one realm to the next without ever testing them.

One example of this is Bloom's (1964) statement that 50 percent of a child's intelligence is developed by 4 years of age. It is true that approximately 50 percent of the variability in individual differences in IQ measured at 18 years can be seen in IQ scores at 4 years, but Bloom's overgeneralization completely ignores the possibility that a particular child may increase many fold the amount of information, processing facility, and new skills he or she learns between 4 and 18 years of age. Another example of overgeneralization concerns the area of behavioral genetics, which is based on individual differences. But factors that affect individual differences in behavior may or may not determine developmental functions. Most developmentalists believe that early mental development is closely governed by maturational (that is, genetic) factors, yet the evidence for the heritability of early mental performance is very slim (McCall, 1970, 1972, 1979a; but see Wilson, 1972, 1978, for an epigenetic perspective). While a general developmental function plotted for a species may be highly genetic, individual differences within that function are not—at least until early childhood.

If we are going to fully understand developmental processes, we cannot confine our study to consistency and ignore change, and we cannot isolate ourselves within one realm of development or another. I believe we must search for change at least as vigorously as we search for consistency and do so within the realms of both developmental functions and individual differences. Then we must regard evidence from each realm as supplying potentially independent pieces of the same puzzle.

Studying Transitions in Early Mental Development

Unfortunately, we developmentalists have held allegiances to consistency and to one or another realm for so long that we do not have a ready arsenal of methods and statistical techniques to study change simultaneously in both realms. Neither do we collect data or construct theories with the idea of explaining changes in these two realms. Even Piaget, who does emphasize change, focuses entirely on the developmental function and essentially ignores individual differences. Strategically, we have two options in studying change: We can start afresh with new data collected from research designed to reveal change in both realms, or we can take old data collected for other purposes and reanalyze it from the perspective of change. The former option is ideal, but it requires a considerable investment of time and money. Thus I chose the second research strategy as an initial approach to the problem, although it will necessarily yield more limited conclusions.

The Fels Longitudinal Study. The Fels study contains infant developmental assessments on substantial numbers of subjects throughout the infancy period (McCall and others, 1972). Since subjects were sampled continuously for many years, the ages at which tests were given and the tests themselves changed over the years. Data were available from a large number of subjects, who were tested on the same test, the Gesell scales of infant development, at 6, 12, 18, and 24 months of age. Therefore, a large sample size, typically required for factoring techniques, was achieved, but at the expense of relatively infrequent measurement.

Ideally, one would like to determine the dimensions underlying the set of individual item responses at a given age and observe how those dimensions changed across age — all in a single analysis. While two standard statistical techniques exist to do this, they were inappropriate for these data. The first, three-mode factor analysis (Tucker, 1966), is an extension of the usual factor analysis of a two-dimensional matrix (for example, subjects by items) to include a third dimension (for example, age). Unfortunately, such an analysis requires that the same items exist at each age analyzed. Infant test data do not fulfill this requirement. The other technique, structural equation analysis (Jöreskog, 1979), does permit the inclusion of different items at different ages but also requires specific hypotheses about the factorial structure and relationships among the factors over age. Structural-equation analysis is a hypothesis-testing procedure and therefore is less suitable for the descriptive work required at the initial stages of investigation.

We opted for a third approach that could be used with the data available (McCall and others, 1972). We conducted separate principal-components analyses at each of the four ages to look at the qualitative nature of the developmental function for early mental performance. Then we correlated component scores across age to examine the relative stability of individual differences in specific skill areas as a function of age (McCall and others, 1972). We chose principal-components analysis without rotations that bias the analysis toward a simple type of structure (such as in Varimax) because we wanted simply to boil down the items into separate dimensions while imposing as few restrictions as possible on the data. Had we performed a Varimax rotation, we would have forced individual items to load maximally on one factor and minimally on another. This procedure tends to yield more interpretable factors, but there is no guarantee that nature operates in this way. Principal-components analysis, on the other hand, summarizes the item set with the fewest arbitrary constraints imposed on the data. Lewis and Enright (1978) have since performed a similar study using Varimax rotation, with generally similar results.

Our reanalysis of the Fels data was not the first time infant development test items had been factored (Stott and Ball, 1965), but it was one of the few times that the same babies contributed data at each of several ages — a requirement for a truly developmental study. We found that the change in the first principal components, which represent the predominant theme underlying performance at a given age, reflected *transitions in developmental function*. At 6 months of age, the first principal component reflected visually guided exploration of perceptual contingencies. Major loadings were on items in which the infant's manipulation of an object produced some clear, contingent perceptual consequence. But at 12 months, the main theme in infant performance was a mixture of sensorimotor and social imitation, plus rudimentary vocal-verbal behavior. This finding agreed with Piaget's (1946) hypothesis that imitation mediates the transition between egocentric sensorimotor behaviors and the more decentered, verbal and social behaviors characteristic of child-hood. At 18 months, the first principal component consisted of verbal and motor imitation, verbal production, and verbal comprehension. By 24 months of age, the main performance theme was even more verbal in character, emphasizing verbal labeling, comprehension, fluency, and grammatical maturity. These results suggest discontinuities (qualitative changes) in the developmental function for early mental performance.

Next we looked at whether there was stability or instability in the *individual differences* in subjects' performances across age. The fact that the main developmental function was discontinuous does not necessarily mean that individual differences will be unstable. It is possible that *rate* of development is consistent, such that the individual infants who enter a stage first are also the first ones out of it and into the next stage, even though the stages are defined by qualitatively different behaviors. We therefore correlated component scores for the first principal components at each of the four ages. The correlations were significant for each pair of components for both sexes. Of course, correlations were highest between adjacent ages and lowest across longer age spans. Thus, while the developmental function was discontinuous, individual differences in the behaviors that characterized that function showed modest stability.

The principal-components analyses yielded more than a single component (main performance theme) at each age. The remaining components were analyzed for *minor transitions* in behavior. We correlated all the components across the ages in search of other developmental patterns showing cross-age stability in individual differences. The most remarkable result uncovered was that while both boys and girls showed cross-age stability for the first principal components, there was almost no similarity between the sexes in the patterns of cross-age stabilities involving components other than the first. Here, then, was another lesson: Not only might continuity and discontinuity of developmental function be independent of stability or instability of individual differences, but the relationships between these two realms might be different for separate groups of subjects — in our case, males and females. Specifically, both sexes showed (1) the same primary developmental function, which was discontinuous, (2) the same pattern of modest stability of individual differences across age for that primary function, and (3) the same structure of minor components (that is, the same item composition of components other than the first within each age). However, the two sexes revealed very different patterns of cross-age stability and instability in individual performance in these minor components.

The Berkeley Growth Study. The Fels study provides data from a large number of subjects and so allows the use of factorial procedures, but it has the disadvantage that there were only a few assessments, spaced infrequently in relation to the rate of developmental change that normally occurs in infants. The Berkeley Growth Study, on the other hand, contains data from far fewer subjects who were assessed much more frequently—every month during the first fifteen months, every three months up to 30 months of age and every six months up to 60 months of age (McCall and others, 1977). The more frequent assessment allowed us to search more specifically for points of transition in the qualitative nature of the developmental function and for points of instability across age in individual differences in performance. We looked at whether changes in one realm coincided with changes in the other realm. Furthermore, any common trends we found in the results of the Fels and Berkeley studies would represent replications in behavioral changes identified with different infant tests (that is, the Gesell versus the precursor of the Bayley, which was used in the Berkeley study). In addition, the discovery of such common trends would eliminate change as a confound, because the Fels study contains data sampled continuously across four decades of children, while the Berkeley study represents a single cohort born in 1928-1929.

The Berkeley data were analyzed in essentially the same fashion as those of the Fels study. Principal-components analyses were conducted separately within each age, and component scores were correlated across age (McCall and others, 1977). Major attention was again paid to the qualitative nature of the first principal component at each age and the relative stabilities of individual differences across age on component scores for these first principal components. This time, however, greater concern was paid to any similarities between discontinuities in developmental function and relative instabilities in individual differences in performance.

Our general hypothesis was that if development during infancy proceeds in qualitatively different stages, one should find relative instability—a dip in cross-age correlations—at transition points in the developmental function (that is, at stage boundaries). For example, if different factors govern performance in one stage than in the next stage, then lower cross-age correlations might be found at stage boundaries as a result of this shift in governing factors. Of course, even if there were qualitative shifts in the predominant nature of mental performance, cross-age correlations would not necessarily drop. But if they did, that fact would support the notion that early mental development consists of a sequence of qualitatively different stages governed by somewhat different factors from stage to stage.

We adopted a unique statistical strategy to analyze the stability of individual differences as reflected in the pattern of cross-age correlations. We could have simply plotted the correlation between the first principal component at adjacent ages, locating the point that corresponded to the midpoint of the age intervals spanned by the correlation (for example, the correlation between the principal components at 1 and 2 months would be plotted over the age of 1½ months). But, this direct approach has two liabilities. First, single correlations for small samples of subjects (made even smaller by the fact that males and females may differ in their patterns of cross-age correlations) are relatively unstable, and consequently trends might be difficult to perceive.

Second, we did not know how many months might be involved in one transition period versus another. Infants vary in when they make a stage transition, and that transition might take one, two, or several months to occur. Our strategy, then, was (1) to use a moving average of correlations, rather than single correlations, to smooth out the data, and (2) to calculate the average over short, medium, and long developmental intervals, which were sensitive to transition periods that spanned different lengths of time.

The details of this strategy are illustrated in Figure 1. Suppose this figure represents the correlation matrix for assessments made monthly between 1 and 7 months of age. The main diagonal contains correlations calculated across adjacent months; that is, r_{12} is the correlation between the first principal-component scores at 1 and 2 months, r_{23} represents the correlation between

Figure 1. Calculation of a Moving Mean of
Longitudinal Correlations

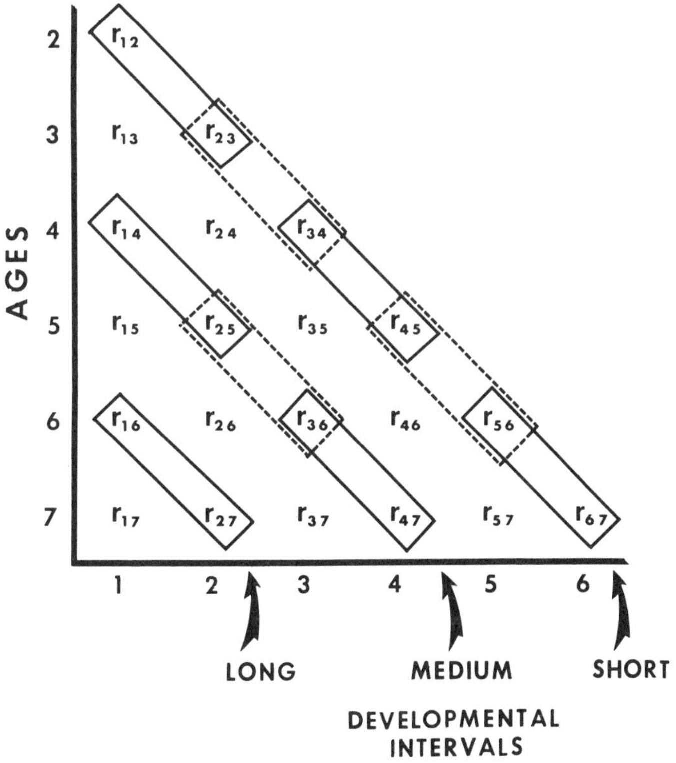

Source: McCall and others, 1977. Reprinted with permission.

first principal-component scores at 2 and 3 months, and so on. We simply averaged adjacent pairs of correlations to smooth out the trend; r_{12} and r_{23} were averaged and plotted over month 2, r_{23} and r_{34} were averaged and plotted over month 3, and so on. The same strategy was used to plot the medium interval diagonal of the correlation matrix: Correlations span three months — r_{14} was averaged with r_{25} and plotted over month 3, and so on. And an analogous procedure was conducted for another diagonal of the matrix that plots correlations between even longer age spans.

The plots of these smoothed correlations, which span short, medium, and long developmental intervals, are shown separately for boys and girls in Figures 2 and 3. We wanted to detect any marked dips in the pattern of correlations across age, regardless of whether these dips occurred in one, two, or all

Figure 2. Relative Stabilities of Individual Differences on the First Principal Components for Females

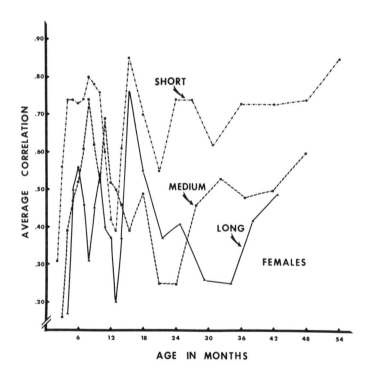

Source: McCall and others, 1977. Reprinted by permission.

Figure 3. Relative Stabilities of Individual Differences on the
First Principal Components for Males

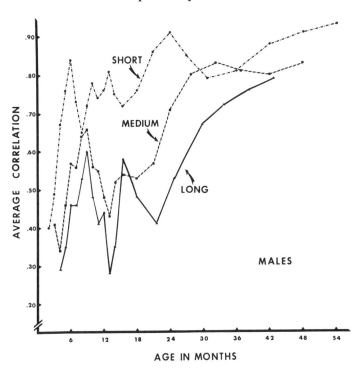

Source: McCall and others, 1977. Reprinted by permission.

three of the time-span plots—and to see whether they were consistent across sex. We did find variations in which plots revealed a dip, but there was also some consistency in the timing of dips in correlations across the sexes. Specifically, cross-age correlations were low until 2 to 4 months of age, and relative instability occurred between 7 and 8 months, 13 and 14 months, and 18 and 21 months for both males and females.

It also appears that these points of instability in individual differences coincided with transitions in developmental function, because the principal components seemed to change their fundamental character at these points more than at other ages. Indeed, the qualitative nature of the stages was very similar to our findings with the Fels data (McCall, 1979b). Specifically, the first principal components at 2 months of age represented responsive attention to particular visual and auditory stimuli and the exercising of inborn motor patterns (Emde and Robinson, 1980; Parmelee and Sigman, 1976). At 3 through 7 months of age the infant's exploration of perceptual contingencies was the main theme underlying performance. Such behaviors were supplemented during the 8 to 13 month period by vocal and elementary verbal behavior as well as by imitation, and the vocal and imitative activities seemed to increase throughout this stage. Then, between 14 and 18 months, two new skills were added—the use of a number of real words in children's vocabulary and the perception of relations between forms. By 21 months, the new skills consisted of constructing and applying rudimentary relationships between symbolic entities.

Are These Really Stages? We admit some ambiguity in the ability of the data to support these conclusions. For example, how much of a dip in the cross-age correlations is significant? Why did these dips not occur more consistently across developmental spans and across sexes? How much of a change from age to age in the character of the behavior components of performance is significant? Are changes in the behavioral components at different ages actually reflected in changes in the *nature* of the test, which are reflected in the use of different items at different ages thereby producing lowered stabilities in individual differences across ages?

All these criticisms are plausible. We believe, however, that we found stages—that is, changes in the predominant character of the developmental function accompanied by points of relative instability in cross-age correlations. The qualitative nature of the stages, as well as the approximate ages of the transition points, seems to coincide with the theoretical positions of Piaget (1952), Uzgiris (1976), and Fischer (1980). In general, the data were consistent with the following stages: endogenous control, 1 to 2 months (Emde and Robinson, 1980; Parmelee and Sigman, 1976); complete subjectivity, 3 to 7 months; separation of means from ends, 7 to 13 months; objectification of environmental entities, 13 to 21 months; and symbolic relations, 21 + months. This conformity to other stage theories was all the more fascinating because the items on the tests used in the Fels and Berkeley studies were not devised or selected with Piaget and these other theorists in mind—in fact, they antedated Piaget.

We also attempted to determine whether points of instability could be found at the hypothesized stage boundaries in other longitudinal data (Wilson and Harpring, 1972) and in the Berkeley data (Bayley, 1933) if another analytic strategy was used (McCall and others, 1977; McCall, 1979b). We hypothesized that if transitions existed at the ages we discerned in the Berkeley data, then correlations across a fixed number of months should be lower if that time span straddled a stage boundary than if that time span was contained only within one stage. The data, which are shown in Table 1, were consistent with this hypothesis, although the differences found were not large. The

Table 1. Average Bayley Test Score Correlations Across Various Age Spans as a Function of Whether or Not Those Spans Are Within a Stage or Cut Across a Stage Boundary

Bayley (1933)[a]	Age Span in Months			
	1	2	3	4-9
Within a stage	.84	.75	.82	.82
Across 1 stage boundary	.80	.74	.77	.68

Wilson and Harpring (1972)[b]	Age Span in Months				
	3	6	9	12	15
Within a stage	.52				
Across 1 stage boundary	.45	.39	.37		
Across 2 stage boundaries			.29	.28	.20

[a]Averages of two to six correlations. Data from one to four months have been omitted because reliability and cross-age rs are known to be low for this period.

[b]Averages of one to four correlations for members of twin pairs.

correlations were lower if they straddled the stage boundary than if they did not, and this seemed to be true for each of the three hypothesized transition points. Given the variability in samples, infant tests, assessment procedures, and other factors, perhaps we should not have expected too much from this analysis. Therefore, it was gratifying that the results were at least consistent with the hypothesis. Of course, these are not the only data that can be marshalled to support our interpretation, and the interested reader is referred to the arguments, reviews, and theory presented in McCall (1979a, 1979b) and McCall and others (1977).

General Conclusions. It is clear from the work presented here that changes in developmental function and in the stability of individual differences can be discerned even with conventional statistics, if one uses them for the purpose of describing change and not just consistency. Moreover, in this particular instance, discontinuities in developmental function coincided with the instability of individual differences in performance, which suggests that new factors control mental performance from one stage to the next. Dips in the cross-age correlations can also be found at stage boundaries, presumably reflecting the existence of some common factors that govern performance from one stage to the next. Perhaps there is a difference in rate of development between individual infants that is relatively consistent across age.

Of course, if we had chosen the one other research strategy for studying change in developmental functions and individual differences—that is, collecting new data for the express purpose of testing for transitions—we would have proceeded much differently. Items that reflected the underlying performance themes hypothesized to characterize a given stage would have been deliberately constructed. We would have made certain that items reflecting a given stage were present in the test battery at ages other than those included in the stage hypothesized to embrace that behavior. Specific scores would have been composed beforehand to measure when specific skills hypothesized to be contained in one stage were present there but not in another. These and other procedures would permit a more discriminating look at the onset and composition of stages and perhaps sharpen our notions of stability and instability of individual differences in performance.

Studying Change in Nonshared, Within-Family, Discontinuous Environmental Variation

The work presented in the previous section describes the stages most infants experience in the course of early mental development. But changes in mental performance can also occur for individuals, not for an entire species, and such changes might happen at nearly any age. Furthermore, stage transitions might be ingrained somewhat in the biological character of the species and fueled by environmental supports for growth that are typically available to nearly all individuals. Yet other changes in mental performance might be more mediated by variable characteristics of the environment, perhaps interacting with genetic dispositions. And while the stages described above represent qualitative changes in development, other changes might be more quantitative in nature. For example, the Fels subjects showed an average range of 28.5 IQ points per individual between 2½ and 17 years of age (McCall and others, 1973). This section will review some attempts to describe quantitative changes, mediated primarily by environmental circumstances, in the mental performance of individual children.

When psychologists begin to list environmental contributions to intelligence, they typically mention the general intellectual climate of the home: parental modeling of language and insistence on its use, parental encouragement of achievement, the availability of experiences that broaden and enrich thought, educational opportunities, and so forth. For the most part, these factors should exert roughly the same influence on all children in the family and tend to make siblings similar to one another. But Rowe and Plomin (1981) suggest that approximately 50 percent of the variance in tested intelligence is environmental — and that approximately half of that environmental variance is due to events that occur within the same family and are not shared by siblings. That is, such environmental variation is not associated with factors that characterize an entire family and have relatively equal impact on all siblings within the family. Therefore, one-half of all the environmental variance in IQ is specific to individual children within a family.

Most of this within-family environmental variance probably will be reflected in changes in mental performance across age. I have attempted to support this proposition by showing that roughly half the variance in IQ between subjects at a single age is associated with within-subject developmental variation (McCall, 1983b). I argue further that a good share of this variance is due to systematic developmental variation within individuals that is not genetic in origin. While my argument is slippery in places, I still believe that a substantial contribution to IQ scores comes from environmental factors we typically ignore — that is, those associated with developmental changes within individuals that are not shared by siblings within a family. These factors may include major environmental events that influence one child within a family differently from another, perhaps as a function of the diverse natures of those children prior to the event. Divorce, for example, may have different effects on the mental performance of a preschooler than on that of a teenager. Birth order may be another factor. Some younger children may simply avoid developing skills possessed by their older brothers and sisters. Also, different children have different teachers, and one child may benefit more from a given teacher than another.

There are very few data linking a specific environmental event with changes in mental performance. One class of studies testing the influence of such an event examines the effects of going to preschool on children of poverty. In comparisons of children experiencing preschools with control children, such special early education produces a temporary increase in IQ, less need for special education classes at later ages, and fewer grade failures (that is, retentions in a grade) throughout the school careers of the special-program children (Lazar and Darlington, 1982).

Another attempt to highlight a nonshared environmental factor is the confluence theory of mental performance (Zajonc and Markus, 1975). A major premise of this theory is that the birth of a younger sibling dilutes the intellectual environment within a family for an older child. Consequently, the birth of a younger sibling should lead to a temporary decline in the relative mental performance of the older child. Ironically, although this premise is crucial to the theory, it has never been tested developmentally. Studies have compared mental performance at a single age for later and earlier born children between and within families, but until recently no one has examined one of the developmental dynamics of the theoretical proposition — that mental performance of the older child should decline for a period of time following the birth of a younger sibling.

I tested this developmental proposition using the Fels data (McCall, 1983a). While the number of subjects was small, control over relevant variables was greater than usual. Subjects were divided into only children, first-borns, and later-borns and matched across certain groups for sex, family size, age at testing, and IQ before the birth of the sibling. Analysis of the data revealed that the birth of a younger child indeed produced a decline of 10 IQ points in the only children and 5 to 6 IQ points in the last-born children in families of comparable size. These differences diminished with age and usually disappeared by age 17. Therefore, certain events that occur within the same family but have effects on individual children that are not shared by siblings are associated with changes in mental performance. Such environmental factors

78

may account for as much as one-fourth of the total variance found in IQ scores and up to one-half of the total environmental variance. Such factors have been ignored to a large extent and deserve more attention.

Summary

Developmental psychology should be the study of change within individuals at different ages. We must search for change at least as vigorously as we pursue consistency. And we must do this within the realms of both developmental functions and individual differences. The studies of change reviewed here relied on existing data collected for other purposes. They were justifiable first attempts, but limited in the amount and specificity of the evidence they could provide for developmental change. Nevertheless, the studies reveal that substantial change occurs in development — much of it in theoretically reasonable ways. In addition, preliminary evidence suggests that large amounts of developmental change reflect within-family environmental factors not shared by siblings, a class of variable heretofore almost completely ignored.

References

Bayley, N. "Mental Growth During the First Three Years: A Developmental Study of 61 Children by Repeated Tests." *Genetic Psychology Monographs*, 1933, *14*, 1–92.

Bloom, B. S. *Stability and Change in Human Characteristics*. New York: Wiley, 1964.

Emde, R. N., and Robinson, J. "The First Two Months: Recent Research in Developmental Psychobiology and the Changing View of the Newborn." In J. Call and R. Noshpitz (Eds.), *Basic Handbook of Child Psychiatry*. New York: Basic Books, 1980.

Fischer, K. W. "A Theory of Cognitive Development: The Control and Construction of Hierarchies of Skills." *Psychological Review*, 1980, *87*, 477–531.

Jöreskog, K. G. "Statistical Estimation of Structural Models in Longitudinal-Developmental Investigations." In J. R. Nesselroade and P. B. Baltes (Eds.), *Longitudinal Research in the Study of Behavior and Development*. New York: Academic Press, 1979.

Lazar, I., and Darlington, R. "Lasting Effects of Early Education: A Report from the Consortium for Longitudinal Studies." *Monographs of the Society for Research in Child Development*, 1982, *47*, entire issue.

Lewis, M. and Enright, M. K. "The Development of Mental Abilities: A Multi-Dimensional Model of Intelligence in Infancy." Paper presented at the meetings of the Eastern Psychological Association, Washington, D.C., April, 1978.

McCall, R. B. "IQ Pattern over Age: Comparisons Among Siblings and Parent-Child Pairs." *Science*, 1970, *170*, 644–648.

McCall, R. B. "Similarity in Developmental Profile Among Related Pairs of Human Infants." *Science*, 1972, *178*, 1004–1005.

McCall, R. B. "Challenges to a Science of Developmental Psychology." *Child Development*, 1977, *48*, 333–344.

McCall, R. B. "The Development of Intellectual Functioning in Infancy and the Prediction of Later IQ." In J. D. Osofsky (Ed.), *Handbook of Infant Development*. New York: Wiley, 1979a.

McCall, R. B. "Qualitative Transitions in Behavioral Development in the First Three Years." In M. H. Bornstein and W. Kessen (Eds.), *Psychological Development from Infancy: Image to Intention*. Hillsdale, N.J.: Erlbaum, 1979b.

McCall, R. B. "Nature-Nurture and the Two Realms of Development: A Proposed Integration with Respect to Mental Development." *Child Development*, 1981, *52*, 1-12.

McCall, R. B. "Developmental Changes in Mental Performance: The Effect of the Birth of a Sibling." Unpublished manuscript, 1983a.

McCall, R. B. "Environmental Effects on Intelligence: The Forgotten Realm of Discontinuous Nonshared Within-Family Factors." *Child Development*, 1983b, *54*, 408-415.

McCall, R. B., Appelbaum, M. I., and Hogarty, P. S. "Developmental Changes in Mental Performance." *Monographs of the Society for Research in Child Development*, 1973, *38*, entire issue.

McCall, R. B., Eichorn, D. H., and Hogarty, P. S. "Transitions in Early Mental Development." *Monographs of the Society for Research in Child Development*, 1977, *42*, entire issue.

McCall, R. B., Hogarty, P. S., and Hurlburt, N. "Transitions in Infant Sensorimotor Development and the Prediction of Childhood IQ." *American Psychologist*, 1972, *27*, 728-748.

Parmelee, A. H., Jr., and Sigman, M. "Development of Visual Behavior and Neurological Organization in Pre-term and Full-term Infants." In A. D. Pick (Ed.), *Minnesota Symposium on Child Psychology*. Vol. 10. Minneapolis: University of Minnesota Press, 1976.

Piaget, J. *The Origins of Intelligence in Children*. (M. Cook, trans.). New York: International Universities Press, 1952.

Rowe, D. C., and Plomin, R. "The Importance of Non-shared (E£) Environmental Influences in Behavioral Development." *Developmental Psychology*, 1981, *17*, 517-531.

Stott, L. H., and Ball, R. S. "Infant and Preschool Mental Tests: Review and Evaluation." *Monographs of the Society for Research in Child Dvelopment*, 1965, *30*, entire issue.

Tucker, L. R. "Learning Theory and Multivariate Experiments: Illustration by Determination of Generalized Learning Curves." In R. B. Cattell (Ed.), *Handbook of Multivariate Experimental Psychology*. Chicago: Rand McNally, 1966.

Uzgiris, I. C. "Organization of Sensorimotor Intelligence." In M. Lewis (Ed.), *Origins of Intelligence*. New York: Plenum, 1976.

Wilson, R. S. "Twins: Early Mental Development." *Science*, 1972, *175*, 914-917.

Wilson, R. S. "Synchronies in Mental Development: An Epigenetic Perspective." *Science*, 1978, *202*, 939-948.

Wilson, R. S., and Harpring, E. B. "Mental and Motor Development in Infant Twins." *Developmental Psychology*, 1972, *7*, 227-287.

Wohlwill, J. F. *The Study of Behavioral Development*. New York: Academic Press, 1973.

Zajonc, R. B., and Markus, G. B. "Birth Order and Intellectual Development." *Psychological Review*, 1975, *82*, 74-88.

Robert B. McCall is senior scientist and science writer at the Boys Town Center in Nebraska. His research interests include cognitive development in infancy and methods for analyzing developmental change in longitudinal data. He is also involved in the communication of research findings from the behavioral sciences to the public via press and television.

*Cognitive-developmental discontinuities seem to occur during
several periods in childhood and adolescence — at 4 to 5, 6 to 7,
10 to 12, and 14 to 16 years.*

Developmental Discontinuities in Childhood and Adolescence

Sheryl L. Kenny

Children's physical growth is usually not striking to people who live with them
day in and day out. Development, whether physical or mental, unfolds gradually and naturally over a long period of time. The fact that development
occurs gradually, however, does not necessarily mean that the *rate* of development is always the same. There are times when a child appears to be learning
at faster or slower rates. Different rates of both physical and mental development have been documented throughout childhood and adolescence (Emde
and others, 1976; Fischer, 1980; McCall, 1979; White, 1970). Some researchers
suggest that new learning occurs mainly during the faster periods of physical
growth (Epstein, 1974), with skill acquisition progressing rapidly during certain high growth periods and then leveling off during slow growth periods.
The approach presented in this chapter does not draw quite so strong a dicho-
tomy between fast and slow periods of development. Instead skills are viewed
as accumulating in an ongoing and continuous process, with spurts in developmental pace marking the emergence of new learning potentials.

Development is therefore both continuous and discontinuous. Individuals experience gradual transitions and stage-like changes in the process of
skill acquisition. Neither aspect can be ignored without losing a piece of the

Preparation of this chapter was supported by a grant from the Carnegie
poration of New York. The statements made and views expressed are solely the r·
sibility of the author. The author gratefully acknowledges the assistance and suₚ
Kurt Fischer and Marilyn Pelot during the preparation of this chapter.

K. W. Fischer (Ed.). *Levels and Transitions in Children's Development.* New Directions
for Child Development, no. 21. San Francisco: Jossey-Bass, September 1983.

total picture of development. Faster periods of development or spurts—
discontinuities—provide a child or adolescent with a new potential for more
complex reasoning. This new potential remains present during slower periods
of growth, as the individual learns new skills and broadens the content of
previously acquired skills (Fischer and Pipp, forthcoming). This chapter will
focus on the evidence for discontinuities in development that occur in
childhood and adolescence and ways to assess these developmental changes.
Before the evidence for these discontinuities is presented, the methods used to
detect developmental changes will be clarified. Inconsistencies that are sometimes present in data and research as a result of the ambiguities of behavior
and of variations in methodology will also be examined. Finally, suggestions
for improved methods to assess development, especially in adolescence, will be
discussed.

Measuring Discontinuities

Since discontinuities involve rapid change or spurts, it is useful to consider how a developmental change fits within the life cycle of an individual.
From the individual's perspective, developmental shifts occur relatively slowly
and gradually. Across the life cycle there are large changes in many skills, but
these changes may often occur too slowly to be considered discontinuous. In
order to be discontinuous, development must advance by large and rapid
qualitative changes. Measurement and detection of these changes requires
special methods (Fischer and others, forthcoming).

One method for detecting discontinuities uses a developmental sequence
in a single skill area. Each task assesses a different step in the sequence, and
the tasks differ minimally in content—varying primarily in terms of the complexity of the behavior required to perform them. With either a longitudinal or
a cross-sectional design, it is possible to use such a scale to determine where
rapid change occurs in the sequence. Some researchers hypothesize that developmental spurts will be consistently evident at certain regions of such a sequence whenever individuals are showing optimal performance—the very best
they can do in that domain (Fischer and Bullock, 1981).

In a study of arithmetic skills, for example, a sequence of arithmetic
tasks was given to children between 8 and 20 years of age (Kenny and Fischer,
in preparation). Each student performed a sequence of tasks designed to test
several of the cognitive-developmental levels posited by skill theory (Fischer,
1980). Level 6 *representational systems* were assessed by tasks that required solutions to a set of simple arithmetic problems (for example, $5 + 7 = ?$) as well as
concrete verbal explanations of the solutions. Tasks were administered for
each of the four basic arithmetic operations—addition, subtraction, multiplication, and division. Tasks for Level 7 *single abstractions* consisted of the same
problems but required an abstract definition of the relevant arithmetic operation: That is, the response had to explain the operation adequately in a com-

plete sentence in general terms; it could not merely refer to the specific numbers in the problem.

Level 8 *abstract mappings*, which involve simple relations between two or more abstractions, were assessed by tasks of the following type: Students were given two arithmetic problems representing two related operations and then asked to answer the specific problems and explain in general how the operations are related as illustrated by the problems. For example, the following pair of problems deals with the relation between addition and multiplication: $6 \times 4 = ?$ and $6 + 6 + 6 + 6 = ?$ Preliminary data have also been collected to assess performance at Levels 9 and 10. The tasks for Level 9 *abstract systems* were similar to those for Level 8 in that they involved relations between two arithmetic operations, but the relations between the operations were distant or indirect, as in the relation between addition and division. The tasks for Level 10 required explanation of a general principle relating all four operations.

Developmental discontinuities or spurts were predicted for optimal performance on the tasks for each level. Optimal performance was induced by the provision of instruction and practice with the tasks. For each task students were shown a good answer and allowed to study it briefly. Two weeks later, they were tested again, after they had the opportunity to work on the tasks and think about them. In a cross-sectional design like the one used in this study, one measure of discontinuity is the occurrence of bimodal distributions of performances. Gradual development would produce a broad distribution of performances, probably fitting something like a normal curve. Developmental discontinuities or spurts, on the other hand, would lead most subjects to either pass virtually all tasks or fail virtually all of them.

The results strongly demonstrated discontinuity. Scores showed striking bimodal distributions for optimal performance, with virtually all individuals either passing or failing nearly all the tasks for a given level (Fischer and others, forthcoming). Because the sample did not include children young enough to lack the capacity for Level 6 tasks, the data provided complete tests for only Levels 7 and 8. For each of those levels, the bimodal distribution was distinct, with Level 7 skills spurting at 10-to-11 years of age and Level 8 skills at 16 years.

According to the optimal-level hypothesis, there are upper limits on an individual's ability to control increasingly complex skills, and movement of the upper limit to a new developmental level coincides with spurts in developmental change (Fischer and Pipp, forthcoming). When a new level emerges, a spurt occurs for skills that are performed optimally, such as those that are used most often. For example, at approximately 10-to-12 years of age, adolescents begin to think abstractly about a number of issues. Before this time, their thoughts are bound by concrete concepts, but during this later developmental period adolescents start to demonstrate abstract concepts that involve such things as politics, school subjects, morality, and the self (Adelson, 1972; Biggs and Collis, 1982; Rosenberg, 1979; Selman, 1980). Optimal performance of tasks involving these abstract concepts is predicted to show rapid development during this period, similar to the finding that arithmetic abstractions begin at 10 to 11 years of age.

Evidence for such spurts in performance associated with cognitive-developmental levels is beginning to accumulate. The data reported in the chapters in this sourcebook by Emde and Lampl, Zelazo and Leonard, Corrigan, and McCall support the existence of spurts during certain age regions in infancy. In addition, a few other studies clearly indicate the occurrence of spurts for developmental levels in childhood and adolescence. For example, Jaques and others (1978) report several examples of discontinuities in performance, including not only bimodal but multimodal distributions of scores that correspond to five predicted levels of abstract reasoning. Embedded within the definition of each level are the appropriate number of thinking modes—five modes for Level 5, four modes for Level 4, and so on. Individuals who reach a particular level can use all modes of reasoning from earlier levels as well. Clusterings of subjects' performances on problem-solving tasks provided evidence for the separate modes of functioning. Multimodal distributions occurred in each age group of subjects tested, and the clusterings coincided with the predicted modes of functioning. For instance, distributions of scores for subjects 17-to-21 years old produced four clusterings that coincided with the four modes of reasoning predicted to exist at Level 4 in the Jaques and others (1978) theory. Very few individuals under age 17 could solve the Level 4 problems. Perhaps this level is equivalent to the one that emerged at 16-to-17 years of age in the study of abstractions in arithmetic, in which subjects were able to describe the relation between two similar operations. One important aside regarding the Jaques study is that distributions of scores were stable for the samples of subjects tested but unstable for individuals. The authors suggest that the instability of individual scores may have resulted from a lack of experience with the unfamiliar tasks.

In a study by Tabor and Kendler (1981), both continuous and discontinuous developmental changes were demonstrated in children ranging from kindergarten through sixth grade. One type of task produced bimodal distributions of scores, while another produced unimodal distributions. Tabor and Kendler interpreted bimodality as evidence of discontinuous development and unimodality as evidence of gradual or continuous development. The discontinuity in task performance occurred at 6-to-7 years of age. Bimodal distributions occurred on a set of class-inclusion tasks, in which children chose the dimension on which the majority of a group of objects were similar. Some individuals passed all or almost all the tasks, while others passed none of them at a particular level. Unimodal distributions occurred on a set of optional-shift tasks, in which children were asked on two separate occasions to discriminate the salient dimension in a set of objects. A tendency to reverse the salient dimension on the second occasion increased with age, but there was no evidence for any discontinuity or spurt.

Why the difference in the patterns of data? The answer to this question may help clarify the inconsistencies that frequently appear in developmental research. The optional-shift tasks did not have a right or wrong answer, in contrast to the class-inclusion tasks. Reversing or not reversing the salient dimension from one occasion to the next was partially a matter of preference. Even though the preference for reversal seemed to increase with age, the task did not provide a good assessment of discontinuous developmental change because it relied on preference in addition to actual ability. Also, in accord with the optimal-level hypothesis, practice on the class-inclusion task tended to improve performance dramatically for some children and not others, producing a bimodal distribution. This same pattern did not occur in the optional-shift task, possibly because of its ambiguous nature. Typically, an ambiguous or highly complicated task will not reflect discontinuities even with practice (Fischer and Corrigan, 1981). In fact, when individuals are given tasks that are complicated for them, they may perform at a much lower level on the complex tasks than their capabilities allow on simpler tasks (Fischer and others, forthcoming; Roberts, 1981).

In conclusion, clearcut discontinuities as evidenced by bimodal distributions seem to occur when the tasks are familiar and have been practiced and when they are simple tests of the ability hypothesized for a developmental level. Environmental conditions also play a crucial supporting or constraining role in the occurrence of discontinuities. Before an optimal level of performance can be detected, the individual must have sufficient environmental support for learning the task (Hand, 1981). The degree of environmental support and the complexity of tasks prove to be two important reasons for the *inconsistencies* in developmental data and theory. But first a look at some of the *consistencies*.

Consistencies in Theory and Data

There seems to be some consensus in the developmental literature about the ages when spurts and plateaus in performance appear. Data and theory indicate major shifts in the reasoning patterns of children and adolescents at 4-to-5, 6-to-7, 10-to-12, and 14-to-16 years of age (Biggs and Collis, 1982; Case, 1980; Fischer, 1980; Halford, 1982; Jacques and others, 1978). Of course, the existence of discontinuities does not depend on all children showing spurts at the same ages, but general age ranges or regions do denote the times when spurts are most likely to first appear. Researchers are largely in agreement concerning the timing of spurts in childhood, preadolescence, and adolescence, as shown in Table 1, but consensus about the timing of changes in late adolescence and early adulthood is not as strong (Basseches, 1980; Broughton, 1978; Kitchener, 1983).

Discontinuous Changes in Childhood. For the childhood years, shifts at 4-to-5 and 6-to-7 years of age are posited frequently. Around age 4, chil-

Table 1. Approximate Ages at Which New Cognitive Levels Are Postulated to Emerge in Several Theories

Age	Skill Theory	Piaget	Broughton	Case	SOLO Taxonomy	Epstein	Jaques et al.	Lee	Kitchener	Selman
1										
2										2–3
3						2–4				
4	4–5		4	4½	4–5		4–5			4–5
5								5–6		
6	6–7					6–8	6–7			6–7
7		7–8			7–8					
8			8							
9										
10										10–11
11	10–12	10–12		11	10–12	10–12	10–12	11		
12			12							
13					13–15					13–15
14	14–16							14		
15						14–16			15–17	
16					16–18					
17										17
18	18–20		18							
19							17–21			
20										
21									20–22	
22										
23									23 +	
24										
25	24–26		25							
26										

Note: The approximate age levels indicated are for childhood and adolescence; infancy has been omitted. The author accepts full responsibility for the interpretation of data presented in the following articles: Skill Theory (Fischer, 1980); Piaget (1970); Case (1980); SOLO Taxonomy (Biggs and Collis, 1982); Epstein (1974); Jaques and others (1978); Lee (1971); Kitchener (1983); Selman (1980).

dren begin to understand simple relations between representations for concrete objects, according to Biggs and Collis (1982), Case (1980), Fischer (1980), Halford (1982), and Siegler (1981). For example, they can understand social roles because they are able to relate complementary behavioral roles such as those of doctor and patient (Watson and Fischer, 1980). Children at this age can also think about the relationships among a variety of objects or concrete ideas. Case's (1980) theory predicts that a spurt or "learning explosion" will occur at $4\frac{1}{2}$ to 5 years of age. Increased memory capacity leads to the ability to form relationships between two pieces of representational knowledge and thus provides the basis for a period of rapid acquisition of knowledge. Marked increases in performance have been reported for this age period in several domains, including number concepts, language abilities, and social roles (for example, Luria, 1961). On the other hand, according to Piaget (1970), thought at this time is still based on direct perceptual information and remains intuitive and egocentric, therefore showing a distinct absence of logical reasoning.

Several theorists propose another developmental level at 6 or 7 years of age (Biggs and Collis, 1982; Fischer, 1980; Piaget, 1970; Tabor and Kendler, 1981; White, 1970). Generally, children at this age become able to coordinate complex concrete or representational skills. Piaget (1970) attributes their ability to focus on and coordinate several concrete relations to the process of decentration. That is, because of their use of concrete operations, children start to rely more on logical relations than immediate perceptual information. Bruner and Kenney (1966) found, for example, that 5-year-olds could reproduce but not transpose a matrix requiring "multiplication" of two dimensions of classification. At age 7, about 80 percent of the children could accomplish both tasks. The same developmental pattern is true for social cognition. Children can coordinate dual social roles for two interacting agents—for example, making an adult doll act simultaneously as both parent and doctor to a child doll. Before age 6, few children are able to coordinate such an intersection of roles (Watson and Fischer, 1980).

A Discontinuous Change in Preadolescence. Another transition in behavioral organization appears around the age of 10-to-12 years, when preadolescents begin to think about abstract concepts in many domains (Biggs and Collis, 1982; Case, 1980; Fischer and others, forthcoming; Halford, 1982; Jaques and others, 1978). Piaget (1970) describes this conceptual change as a movement into the use of formal operations. For the first time, logical thinking about hypothetical situations appears, and children at this age are supposedly able to reason hypothetically in many domains. Piaget's idea of a general formal structure of reasoning has been challenged, since much unevenness in development across domains has been demonstrated empirically (Neimark, 1975). The child's environment seems to have much more influence on this reasoning pattern than the Piagetian framework suggests (Fischer, 1980).

Case (1980) describes formal-reasoning substages that predominate after age 10-to-12. During preadolesence, individuals consolidate their concrete operational skills and shift to formal or abstract operations. Movement to this stage depends upon the expansion of functional working memory to a point where formal operations can begin. After that point in the development of reasoning skills is reached, working memory gradually increases during adolescence and produces the substages of formal reasoning. Skill theory (Fischer, 1980) also describes the emergence at around age 10 of a major behavioral reorganization or cycle of levels called the *abstract tier*. Preadolescents develop the capacity to use Level 7 simple abstractions, which arise from the coordination of two or more concrete representational systems. In skill theory, this level and all others are not stages in the strong Piagetian sense but represent upperbounds on performance of tasks at that level (Bullock, 1981). Additional levels in the abstract tier develop in adolescence and early adulthood and are described in the next two sections.

In Biggs and Collis's (1982) approach, called the SOLO taxonomy (Structure of the Observed Learning Outcome), a reorganization occurs that is similar to skill theory's Level 7. At 10-to-12 years of age, the preadolescent begins to use concrete generalizations, which seem to be identical to single abstractions. They are called "concrete" because they arise from concrete instances, which is also true of skill theory's abstractions. In all three approaches discussed here, Case's model, skill theory, and the SOLO taxonomy, abstract thought is hypothesized to emerge in simple form at 10-to-12 years of age. The new level is built upon earlier concrete or representational abilities, but it involves a reorganization in the structure of thought. Thus, the level is not simply the result of an accumulation of information, although such accumulation does play an important role in cognitive development.

The shift in preadolescence from concrete to abstract thought is evident in numerous data sets. Students are able to begin understanding abstract concepts that involve morality, politics, and personality (Colby and others, 1983; Lee, 1971; Rosenberg, 1979; Selman, 1980), even though they may not be able to reason abstractly about most scientific tasks at that age (Martarano, 1977; Piaget, 1970).

A Discontinuous Change in Adolescence. Another discontinuity in development appears at approximately 14-to-16 years of age. The spurt at this age is commonly described as a shift in reasoning processes toward dealing with or relating multiple abstract concepts. That is, the development of formal reasoning is not complete at age 11 or 12 and shows another major surge in growth a few years later, when complex forms of abstract reasoning emerge.

In the SOLO taxonomy, individuals attain a multistructural understanding of formal concepts at around age 15 in content areas such as mathematics and history (Biggs and Collis, 1982). That is, they can deal with several abstractions or formal concepts simultaneously. According to skill theory, the new level that emerges during this period involves the ability to relate two or more abstract concepts in what are called abstract mappings (Fischer, 1980). Several studies based on skill theory have provided evidence for a spurt in the ability to produce abstract mappings between 14 and 16 years of age (Fischer and others, forthcoming), as described earlier in the arithmetic study (Kenny and Fischer, in preparation). During this age period, Arlin (1975) also found an increase in problem-finding ability—the capacity to consider how to reason about problems. This capacity is similar to the scientist's ability to generate hypotheses in order to explain a set of observations.

Several researchers have distinguished two levels of formal operations. According to Martarano (1977), the use of early formal operations in preadoescence requires only the testing of a hypothesis, but the use of late formal operations in adolescence requires a generalized rule about a hypothesis. In this study, a significant difference occurred between formal-operational scores for eighth- and tenth-graders, suggesting a developmental spurt in performance between these ages. The apparent spurt may have resulted from "differential levels of cognitive development in the formal operational schemata tested" (p. 672). Similarly, Hoemann and Ross (1983) report a marked increase in scores on a formal-operational task in adolescence. After receiving instruction on a proportional-reasoning task, 14-to-15½-year-olds performed well above chance, while 10- to 12-year-olds scored well below chance. Hoemann and Ross suggest that the proportional-reasoning tasks measured a higher level of formal-operational thinking because they "required subjects to combine information from two sources" (p. 116). Jaques and others (1978) also distinguish several types of formal reasoning and find evidence for a spurt at 16-to-17 years in the ability to carry out formal reasoning about multiple concepts.

Several other researchers have collected data that indicate a spurt in adolescence in social-cognitive development. Scores on a set of moral stories used by Lee (1971) showed dramatic spurts at ages 5-to-6, 11, and 14, with plateaus in performance occurring at ages 6-to-10, 12-to-13, and 15. Selman (1980) measured the understanding of interpersonal relationships and found spurts in scores on his Interpersonal Maturity Scale at 10-to-11 and 13-to-15 years, although he did not discuss the spurts.

Discontinuous Changes Beyond Adolescence. Agreement about the timing of discontinuities after the spurt in reasoning abilities at 15 years of age is not as strong. Based on skill theory, Fischer and others (forthcoming) propose two spurts after age 15—one between ages 19 and 21 and another between 24 and 26 years. The spurt at 19-to-21 years reflects the emergence of Level 9 *abstract systems*, in which the individual integrates multiple abstractions in complex relations to form a system of thought, such as the system required to relate the arithmetic operations of addition and division. The spurt at 24-to-26 years involves the emergence of Level 10 *general principles*, in which the individual coordinates two or more abstract systems in terms of some higher-order rule, such as the principle integrating the four arithmetic operations of addition, subtraction, multiplication, and division. Some data support the existence of a developmental spurt at approximately age 20, but few studies have been conducted to test for the existence of the hypothesized spurt at 25 years.

A number of studies do clearly demonstrate, however, that cognitive development continues into early adulthood. In assessments of critical, reflective judgment, Kitchener and King (1981) found significant differences between the forms of judgment used by high school juniors, college juniors, and graduate students. High school juniors tended to think in terms of absolute rights and wrongs. College juniors often made decisions based on the belief that there are no absolute rights and wrongs but only relatively arbitrary beliefs. Graduate students frequently made judgments founded on concepts about close approximations of right and wrong. These findings are similar to those of Perry (1970), who found analogous shifts in reasoning during the college years. Basseches (1980) also reports that undergraduates, graduate students, and college faculty exhibit qualitatively different responses on a measure of dialectical thinking. And Broughton (1978) found changes in reasoning about the self during late adolescence and early adulthood.

Consensus about the timing of spurts seems to decrease as researchers study older samples. The lack of consensus may be due to the small number of systematic studies in the literature or to problems with the methods devised for studying this age group. It is also possible that as individuals grow older, the nature of development changes, becoming less uniform and increasingly differentiated, and thus there may be less consistency in the cognitive-developmental changes that occur in different people.

Inconsistencies in Theory and Data

Although the previous section concerned consistencies in theory and data on developmental discontinuities, consensus is not the norm. In fact, there are many inconsistencies in the evidence collected to date on discontinuities. These inconsistencies seem to result from two pervasive problems: (1) There are difficulties inherent in the study of development in adolescents and adults; (2) different investigators use widely varying methods to assess cognitive development in research done with all age groups, and so it is difficult to compare results across studies.

Problems in Assessing Adolescent Development — and Some Solutions. Because the type of behavior that emerges in adolescence involves thinking with abstract and hypothetical concepts, it is less open to direct observation than the more concrete behaviors that develop at earlier ages. Consequently, performance in adolescents and adults can be easily misinterpreted (Fischer and others, forthcoming). Infants' capabilities, in contrast, are based on sensorimotor actions, which are relatively easy to observe. Behavior in childhood is composed of a combination of sensorimotor actions and mental representations of concrete things in the world. But much of the behavior of adolescents and adults deals with intangible categories and so is several steps removed from directly observable behavior that involves concrete objects and events. Because of this distance from the concrete world, interpretation of the behavior of adolescents and adults can be difficult. For example, the same sentences expressed by different individuals can have very different meanings for assignment of developmental levels—meanings that cannot be detected from the sentences alone.

These ambiguities inherent in adolescent and adult behavior can be substantially reduced by the use of tasks structured to elicit a particular ability and contexts designed to promote the use of that ability. By analyzing the structure of a task, specifying the skills that are needed to successfully complete the task, and devising procedures that evoke behaviors rich enough to allow the detection of those skills, the researcher can reduce the possibilities for alternative interpretations of performance.

But another reason that the behavior of adolescents and adults can be difficult to interpret lies in the immense variation and unevenness in thought and experience in the teenage and adult years. The effect of environmental diversity on individuals seems to increase with age. Middle-class infants and children are, as a group, exposed to similar environments—that is, similar homes, schools, and peer groups. On the other hand, adolescents and young adults in particular encounter a greater variety of situations. Different work experiences, relationships with friends, and educational experiences lead to the accumulation of specialized knowledge from diverse settings. Since individual variation in experience is so large after a certain age, researchers probably should not expect to find broad stages or structures of thinking that apply to adolescent and adult development in a wide range of domains.

To deal with this variability, researchers can focus on specific skill domains and analyze their development in some detail, thus obtaining a useful portrait of development for those specific areas of performance. And, to determine the *degree* to which patterns of development generalize across contexts, the researcher can also sample a range of skills in diverse domains. The use of developmental scales to measure an individual's understanding of, for example, a range of physics problems, family relationships, and religious concepts allows determination of the upper limit on his or her thinking ability across these domains. This upper limit on performance may show developmental discontinuities, despite the unevenness and ambiguity of adolescent and adult behavior (Fischer and Bullock, 1981).

Inconsistencies Due to Varying Research Methods. Variations in design and methodology in developmental research also produce inconsistencies in results, since methods often differ unsystematically from study to study. Some investigators have used open-ended interviews, while others have used highly structured tasks. Some have examined familiar or well practiced skills, while others have examined performance with relatively unfamiliar materials and settings. Other differences involve task complexity, testing environment, and content. Such variations in methodology characterize not only research on adolescents and adults but also research on development in general.

Researchers should begin investigating the variations in behavior produced by different methods (Hand, 1981). Studying the effects on performance of a range of contexts and methods would seem to be especially helpful in portraying the complexities of development in adolescents and adults, who in any one sample, normally show a wide range of developmental levels. At the same time, researchers must select methods that will maximize their ability to test developmental hypotheses. Some of the most promising methods for this purpose at present seem to be task analysis, the minimum-task rule, scalogram techniques, practice and instruction procedures, and the systematic sampling of experimental conditions.

Methodologies based on task analysis pinpoint the behaviors that are necessary to demonstrate understanding of a concept. When tasks are designed to specifically elicit certain behaviors, the ambiguities found in the resulting behaviors are minimized. In our study of arithmetic concepts, the students were given a card with a prototypical answer for each task (Kenny and Fischer, in preparation). These answers were derived from careful task analyses and provided a form of instruction that helped students understand the concepts and give the best responses they could. In general, careful definition of prototypical behaviors for a developmental level on a given task would make it easier both to assess the level and to obtain optimal performance.

Task complexity also seems to have an impact on the ability to detect discontinuities in development. The most straightforward and simplest tasks possible for assessing the skill under study appear to provide the least ambiguous results. Abiding by this minimum-task rule decreases the chance of underestimating individuals' skills because of unnecessarily complicated tasks (Fischer, 1980; Roberts, 1981).

One way of dealing with both task analysis and task complexity is to use multiple tasks to assess development instead of merely one task. A particularly powerful form of the multiple-task approach is the strong scalogram method, in which a separate task is designed to measure each step in a developmental sequence. With this method the researcher can directly analyze success and failure at each step in the sequence instead of counting on one task to differentiate all steps. The separate analysis of each step provides internal checks on task analyses and task complexity and produces a developmental scale with powerful measurement properties for analyzing developmental change (Fischer and others, forthcoming; Siegler, 1981).

Assessment of the effects of practice and instruction on performance can also provide useful information about discontinuities. Results from several recent studies suggest that practice or instruction may provide a simple method for assessing the upper limit on performance (Hoemann and Ross, 1983; Kenny and Fischer, in preparation; O'Brien and Overton, 1982). Changes in this upper limit may be the most fruitful place to search for developmental discontinuities.

A sampling of both structured and spontaneous assessments also enables the researcher to describe development with some precision. Studying behavior as it occurs naturally—with minimal constraints—can provide a useful portrait of the preferences and strengths of individuals. But spontaneous assessments may also fail to provide an accurate picture of an individual's capacities. Structured assessments, in which irrelevant contextual factors are held constant, can improve the accuracy of the assessment of such capacities. Therefore, a combination of the two types of assessments yields richer data— measuring both competency and preference accurately (Hand, 1981).

Summary

In general, cognitive development is both continuous and discontinuous. Specifically, discontinuities in development seem to occur at several age periods in childhood and adolescence: at 4-to-5, 6-to-7, 10-to-12, and 14-to-16 years of age. Both theory and data show some consensus about when these periods of discontinuity occur.

Methodological variations in development studies seem to account for many of the apparent inconsistencies in the data on discontinuities. In general, the unsystematic use of diverse methods makes it difficult to evaluate the evidence for discontinuities in childhood and adolescence. In adolescent and adult behavior, the natural ambiguity and high variability may help explain the apparent lack of consensus about discontinuities in development after the age of 16. Some valuable techniques that may get rid of some of the inconsistencies found in the research include task analysis, the minimum-task rule, scalogram analysis, sampling of both spontaneous and structured assessments, and practice or instruction. In any case, the field of developmental science needs to begin a methodological housecleaning. Researchers must start refining their assessments in order to produce a fuller, more accurate description of the way development proceeds.

References

Adelson, J. "The Political Imagination of the Adolescent." In J. Kagan and R. Coles (Eds.), *Twelve to Sixteen: Early Adolescence.* New York: Norton, 1972.

Arlin, P. K. "Cognitive Development in Adulthood: A Fifth Stage?" *Developmental Psychology,* 1975, *11,* 602–606.

Basseches, M. "Dialectical Schemata: A Framework for the Empirical Study of the Development of Dialectical Thinking." *Human Development,* 1980, *23,* 400–421.

Biggs, J. B., and Collis, K. F. *Evaluating the Quality of Learning: The SOLO Taxonomy.* New York: Academic Press, 1982.

Broughton, J. "Development of Concepts of Self, Mind, Reality, and Knowledge." In W. Damon (Ed.), *Social Cognition.* New Directions for Child Development, no. 1. San Francisco: Jossey-Bass, 1978.

Bruner, J. S., and Kenney, H. J. "On Multiple Ordering." In J. S. Bruner, R. R. Olver, and P. M. Greenfield (Eds.), *Studies in Cognitive Growth.* New York: Wiley, 1966.

94

Bullock, D. "On the Current and Potential Scope of Generative Theories of Cognitive Development." In K. W. Fischer (Ed.), *Cognitive Development.* New Directions for Child Development, no. 12. San Francisco: Jossey-Bass, 1981.

Case, R. "The Underlying Mechanism of Intellectual Development." In J. R. Kirby and J. B. Biggs (Eds.), *Cognition, Development, and Instruction.* New York: Academic Press, 1980.

Colby, A., Kohlberg, L., Gibbs, J., and Lieberman, M. "A Longitudinal Study of Moral Judgment." *Monographs of the Society for Research in Child Development,* 1983, *48,* entire issue.

Emde, R., Gaensbauer, T., and Harmon, R. "Emotional Expression in Infancy: A Biobehavioral Study." *Psychological Issues,* 1976, *10* (37), entire issue.

Epstein, H. T. "Phrenoblysis: Special Brain and Mind Growth Periods, II: Human Mental Development." *Developmental Psychobiology,* 1974, *7,* 217–224.

Fischer, K. W. "A Theory of Cognitive Development: The Control and Construction of Hierarchies of Skills." *Psychological Review,* 1980, *87* (6), 477–531.

Fischer, K. W., and Bullock, D. "Patterns of Data: Sequence, Synchrony, and Constraint in Cognitive Development." In K. W. Fischer (Ed.), *Cognitive Development.* New Directions for Child Development, no. 12. San Francisco: Jossey-Bass, 1981.

Fischer, K. W., and Corrigan, R. "A Skill Approach to Language Development." In R. E. Stark (Ed.), *Language Behavior in Infancy and Early Childhood.* Amsterdam: Elsevier, 1981.

Fischer, K. W., Hand, H. H., and Russell, S. L. "The Development of Abstractions in Adolescence and Adulthood." In M. Commons, F. Richards, and C. Armon (Eds.), *Beyond Formal Operations.* New York: Praeger, forthcoming.

Fischer, K. W., and Pipp, S. L. "Processes of Cognitive Development: Optimal Level and Skill Acquisition." In R. Sternberg (Ed.), *Mechanisms of Cognitive Development.* San Francisco: Freeman, forthcoming.

Fischer, K. W., Pipp, S. L., and Bullock, D. "Detecting Developmental Discontinuities: Method and Measurement." In R. Harmon and R. N. Emde (Eds.), *Continuities and Discontinuities in Development.* New York: Plenum, forthcoming.

Halford, G. S. *The Development of Thought.* Hillsdale, N.J.: Erlbaum, 1982.

Hand, H. H. "The Relation Between Developmental Level and Spontaneous Behavior: The Importance of Sampling Contexts." In K. W. Fischer (Ed.), *Cognitive Development.* New Directions for Child Development, no. 12. San Francisco: Jossey-Bass, 1981.

Hoemann, H. W., and Ross, B. M. "Children's Concepts of Chance and Probability." In C. Brainerd (Ed.), *Children's Logical and Mathematical Cognition.* New York: Springer-Verlag, 1983.

Jaques, E., with Gibson, R. O., and Isaac, D. J. *Levels of Abstraction in Logic and Human Action.* London: Heinemann, 1978.

Kenny, S. L., and Fischer, K. W. "Optimal Levels in the Development of Abstractions in Arithmetic." Manuscript in preparation. Department of Psychology, University of Denver.

Kitchener, K. S. "Human Development and the College Campus: Sequences and Tasks." In G. Hanson (Ed.), *Assessing Student Development.* New Directions for Student Services, no. 20. Jossey-Bass, 1983.

Kitchener, K. S., and King, P. M. "Reflective Judgment: Concepts of Justification and Their Relationship to Age and Education." *Journal of Applied Developmental Psychology,* 1981, *2,* 89–116.

Lee, L. C. "The Concomitant Development of Cognitive and Moral Modes of Thought: A Test of Selected Deductions from Piaget's Theory." *Genetic Psychology Monographs,* 1971, *83,* 93–146.

Luria, A. R. *The Role of Speech in the Regulation of Normal and Abnormal Behavior.* New York: Liveright, 1961.

McCall, R. B. "Qualitative Transitions in Behavioral Development in the First Two Years of Life." In M. H. Bornstein and W. Kessen (Eds.), *Psychological Development from Infancy: Image to Intention.* Hillsdale, N.J.: Erlbaum, 1979.

Martarano, S. C. "A Developmental Analysis of Performance on Piaget's Formal Operations Tasks." *Developmental Psychology,* 1977, *13,* 666–672.

Neimark, H. "Intellectual Development During Adolescence." In F. D. Horowitz (Ed.), *Review of Child Developmental Research.* Vol. 4. Chicago: University of Chicago Press, 1975.

O'Brien, D., and Overton, W. F. "Conditional Reasoning and the Competence-Performance Issue: A Developmental Analysis of a Training Task." *Journal of Experimental Child Psychology,* 1982, *34,* 274–290.

Perry, W. G., Jr. *Forms of Intellectual and Ethical Development in the College Years: A Scheme.* New York: Holt, Rinehart and Winston, 1970.

Piaget, J. "Piaget's Theory." In P. H. Mussen (Ed.), *Carmichael's Manual of Child Psychology.* New York: Wiley, 1970.

Roberts, R. J., Jr. "Errors and the Assessment of Cognitive Development." In K. W. Fischer (Ed.), *Cognitive Development.* New Directions for Child Development, no. 12. San Francisco: Jossey-Bass, 1981.

Rosenberg, M. *Conceiving the Self.* New York: Basic Books, 1979.

Selman, R. L. *The Growth of Interpersonal Understanding: Developmental and Clinical Analyses.* New York: Academic Press, 1980.

Siegler, R. S. "Developmental Sequences Within and Between Concepts." *Monographs of the Society for Research in Child Development,* 1981, *46,* entire issue.

Tabor, L. E., and Kendler, T. S. "Testing for Developmental Continuities or Discontinuities: Class Inclusion and Reversal Shifts." *Developmental Review,* 1981, *1,* 330–343.

Watson, M. W., and Fischer, K. W. "Development of Social Roles in Elicited and Spontaneous Behavior During the Preschool Years." *Developmental Psychology,* 1980, *16,* 483–494.

White, S. H. "Some General Outlines of the Matrix of Developmental Changes Between Five and Seven Years." *Bulletin of the Orton Society,* 1970, *20,* 41–57.

Sheryl L. Kenny is a graduate student in human development at Cornell University. Her research focuses on cognitive development in children and adolescents, and she is especially interested in the learning of mathematics.

Human development may owe its special character to the way cognitive-developmental and social-interactive changes support one another.

Seeking Relations Between Cognitive and Social-Interactive Transitions

Daniel Bullock

Not very long ago cognitive development and social interaction would have been thought to make a rather odd couple. The domain of cognitive development included topics like object permanence, conservation, and performance on balance-beam problems. The domain of social interaction included topics like persuasion, affiliation, and aggression. Today the climate has changed markedly. Several recent volumes (Butterworth and Light, 1982; Olson, 1980) have included papers treating both topics, and textbooks with sections devoted to concurrent treatment (Maccoby, 1980) have begun to appear. Yet old divisions die hard, and a careful reading of the contemporary literature shows that remnants of the old wall between these areas can still be found. One goal of this chapter is to hasten the collapse of these remaining fragments. To that end, the chapter explores relations between social-interactive and cognitive-developmental transitions. The dominant theme in modern studies of cognitive development has been the idea that the skills underlying performance often undergo a transition from one level of organization to another, more

I would like to thank Kurt Fischer and Alison Adams for helpful comments on a prior draft of this chapter.

K. W. Fischer (Ed.). *Levels and Transitions in Children's Development.* New Directions for Child Development, no. 21. San Francisco: Jossey-Bass, September 1983.

complex level of organization. Recently, researchers have begun to notice similar transitions in the organization of social interaction (Kaye, 1982; Kelley and Thibaut, 1978). Are these two types of transition linked, and if so, in what ways?

Examination of the types of linkage leads to three claims which, if valid, build to the conclusion that human development may owe its special character to the way cognitive-developmental and social-interactive changes support one another. The first and second claims are that reorganizations in thinking transform social relations — and changes in social relations facilitate cognitive reorganization. The third claim is that the higher cognitive functions that make human beings unique are socially constituted ones. As will be seen, substantial empirical and logical support exists for each of these proposals.

How Reorganizations in Thinking Transform Social Relations

One way of thinking about how cognitive-developmental transitions might be related to social-interactive transitions is to suppose that the former create the possibility of the latter without directly causing them. Consider an example. One facet of every infant's egocentrism (despite some recent claims to the contrary) is a failure to appreciate that parents have feelings and intentions that can differ from the infant's own. Thus, knowledge of such differences cannot enter as a factor in the infant's social behavior. The infant cannot be blamed justly for purposely hurting another; likewise, the infant cannot blame the mother for having intentions that are contrary to the infant's own. An upward shift in the infant's capacity to process information can alter this situation quite abruptly. Once the child becomes capable of differentiating and comparing the intentions and feelings of self and other, a new type of interaction emerges, one with genuine battles of wills, genuine aggression by the child, but also genuine comforting by the child.

This example assumes that a cognitive-developmental transition can take the form of increasing the child's capacity to construct, differentiate, and compare cognitive structures (Fischer, 1980; Flavell, 1982). Many cognitive-developmental theorists postulate a number of major transitions of this nature during the period between birth and early adulthood. For example, Fischer (1980) postulates nine major transitions and suggests that there may be many more minor ones. Following each transition, cognitive structures of greater complexity can be synthesized. And, whenever such newly constructed or differentiated structures are based on social experience, their emergence can be expected to have a transformative effect on social relations. Indeed, recent research shows this idea to be applicable at least from infancy through adolescence. Qualitative cognitive transitions have been detected in both child-parent and child-peer relations (Kaye, 1982; Fischer and Watson, 1981; Youniss, 1982).

Of course, perceptive parents have always been impressed by relatively sudden changes in the quality of social relations with their children. In fact, parental behavior may serve as a good index of increments in a child's cognitive capacity. The literature on child-rearing is filled with discussions of shifting maturity demands (see Maccoby, 1980), and some researchers (Baumrind, 1967) even classify parents according to whether they strive to impose maturity demands that are appropriate to their child's developmental level. If parents who so strive also succeed, their shifts in demands would be valid indicators of increments in their child's capacity. At least one study has documented a rough coincidence between maturity-demand shifts and child-capacity shifts (Rogoff and others, 1975). But the study of "motherese" has produced the most compelling evidence that parents may accurately detect child-capacity shifts. Because of its role in my main argument, I will examine this evidence in detail here.

The study of "motherese" encompasses the many psycholinguistic studies of shifts in the content of speech that is addressed to children during their primary language development years (that is, the first seven years of life). Unfortunately, the term *motherese* is something of a misnomer; it suggests that mothers use a special language when speaking to their youngsters. In fact, any older person (child or adult) will adjust his or her speech in order to compensate for a particular youngster's level of verbal performance. Moreover, motherese is not a purely linguistic phenomenon. Though speech adjustments typically do involve syntactic changes, such syntactic effects seem to be a secondary result of attempts by speakers to make their speech topically appropriate for, and comprehensible to, the child (see Cross, 1977). Such adjustments also occur in interactions that need not involve language, such as modeling and imitation.

Note now that parental adjustments are made in two directions. First, the mother must make simplifying adjustments in order to speak in a manner appropriate to her child's performance level. However, her child's performance level is naturally variable, so, to function optimally, her speech adjustments must also vary. If all goes well, the child's performance generally improves. Thus, if the mother's speech is to remain level-appropriate, she must make periodic complicating adjustments. Now consider a case in which the mother has just made an upward adjustment in the complexity of her child-directed speech. Can such a shift be taken as a valid index of an immediately prior upward shift in her child's cognitive capacity?

Answering this question requires drawing a careful distinction between performance level and cognitive capacity. Typically, there seems to be some time lag between when a child's capacity to perform a task increases and when the child reaches a level of skilled performance that makes full use of the added capacity in any particular domain (Fischer and Bullock, 1981). Most of the literature on motherese suggests that parents stay one step ahead of the current verbal performance level of their child. Thus, because lags between capacity increments and performance improvements are the rule, there would seem to be only an occasional coincidence between parental shifts and capacity shifts in the child. Nevertheless, the same reasoning can be used to argue that the coincidence between maternal and children's shifts is high whenever the lag between capacity shifts and performance improvements is minimized (Fischer and others, forthcoming). This coincidence should occur when the mother is making adjustments to match a child's performance in a domain where skills are very highly practiced, since constant practice ensures near-capacity performance.

Some supportive evidence for the coincidence between maternal shifts and children's capacity shifts can be found in the existing literature on motherese. Cross (1977) reports data on child-directed speech from a sample of sixteen specially selected mothers. All mothers included in the sample had to have two children who were "well in advance of their age norms in language use and comprehension" (p. 155). Such precociousness can usually be taken as a sign that the children are performing very near the capacity limit for their age group. Thus, any evidence that these mothers shifted their speech content in response to changes in their children's best performance would also be evidence for maternal shifts that are coincident with child-capacity shifts.

The sixteen children in Cross's sample ranged in age only from 19 to 32 months, and the average difference between their mean-length-of-utterance (MLU) scores was only two words. However, Cross was able to demonstrate impressive correlations (many between .65 and .85) between maternal speech adjustments and various measures of child speech. Moreover, the general trend in her data led Cross to emphasize "the mother's sensitivity to the child's receptive abilities and extended production capacity. This combination accounted for the highest correlations. . . . Correlations with the child's MLU, on the other hand, consistently failed to reach the same levels" (p. 167). The mean of all the child's utterance lengths (MLU) was not as good a predictor of maternal shifts as a mean of the 50 longest utterances taken from a sample of 500 utterances. The latter mean should be an excellent index of the child's true capacity or optimal performance level in such a group of linguistically precocious children, and it is impressive that the mothers in Cross's sample appeared to be tracking this variable. In practice, this meant that mothers' "MLUs were on the average less than three morphemes longer than their children's and less than half a morpheme longer than the children's longest utterances" (p. 172).

In summary, cognitive-developmental transitions—in the form of periodic increases in processing capacity—enable the emergence of new cognitive structures. When such structures are based on social experience, their emergence can be expected to transform performance in the domain of social relations. In one area of social relations—linguistic communication—this is indeed the case. Some mothers appear to be highly sensitive to shifts in the complexity of their children's best performances. As a result, these mothers' contingent speech adjustments can themselves serve as valid indicators of recent cognitive capacity shifts in their children.

How Changes in Social Relations Facilitate
Cognitive Development

Work on motherese began in the mid 1960s in reaction to the preformist theories of Chomsky, who argued that social interaction played little role in language development (see Fischer and Bullock, forthcoming). But most researchers who have studied motherese believe that the speech adjustments made by mothers serve the purpose of facilitating communication with the child, which in turn has the effect of speeding up the pace of language development. If so, then motherese and its effects exemplify not only how cognitive development transforms social relations but also how social relations facilitate cognitive development. Of course, facilitating cognitive development can refer either to actually increasing a child's capacity to process information or to helping the child close the gap between his or her current skill level and the potential level allowed by the child's optimal performance capacity. At this point, such facilitation of cognitive development will be defined according to the second meaning: that is, helping the child to realize his or her current cognitive potential by building up more complex structures or skills. It will not mean altering the child's potential itself.

When discussing the importance of social facilitation of cognitive development to human development, it is important to remember the adaptive function served by cognitive development. It is also important to consider a full range of levels of social interaction. Only a consideration of many levels can clarify what is gained in adaptive power by moving from one level of social-interactive organization to another (compare Dennett, 1975). Some progress along these lines can be found in the literature on social learning theory (Bandura, 1971, 1977). Figure 1 illustrates the essential aspects of a common scenario assumed by social learning theorists that involves two individuals. The first has a high level of expertise relative to the second, and the second individual's adaptive task is to approach, as quickly as possible, the high level of expertise possessed by the first. In Figure 1, the second individual, or "apprentice," starts in the lower left-hand corner, separated from the expert by an arbitrary distance of 100 skill components (shown on the vertical axis; the horizontal axis represents time). By acquiring new skills over time, the apprentice moves toward expert status at some rate. The lines in the graph illustrate four different rates of convergence from apprentice to expert status.

The idea I want to explore can now be stated simply. Moving to a higher level of social interaction brings with it an increased rate of convergence. Such an idea has long been implicit in discussions of social learning. For example, Bandura (1971) has often contrasted the slow rate of convergence observed in individuals who receive haphazard feedback from the physical environment to the fast rate of convergence observed when the young organism can observe a model. He has also distinguished between two types of modeling: symbolic, which involves the use of language, and nonsymbolic,

102

Figure 1. Schematic Illustration of Convergence Rates
Under Four Social-Interactive Conditions

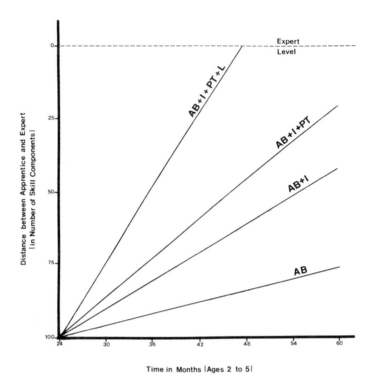

Time in Months (Ages 2 to 5)

which does not. Presumably the convergence rate is faster for individuals involved in symbolic modeling than for those involved in nonsymbolic modeling alone. Thus, in Bandura's scheme there is already an implicit hierarchy of factors that are capable of transforming convergence rate: (1) environmental feedback, (2) nonsymbolic modeling, and (3) symbolic modeling.

By itself, this simple three-step hierarchy illustrates the covariation of convergence rates with levels of social interaction. In the expanded Convergence Rate Hierarchy proposed below, symbolic modeling appears as Level 7 (Language), nonsymbolic modeling as Level 5 (Imitation), and environmental feedback as Level 3 (Operant Conditioning).

1. Natural Selection of Reflexes (NS).
2. NS + Classical Conditioning (CC).
3. NS + CC + Operant Conditioning (OC).

4. NS + CC + OC + Affective Bond (AB).
5. NS + CC + OC + AB + Imitation (I).
6. NS + CC + OC + AB + I + Purposive Teaching (PT).
7. NS + CC + OC + AB + I + PT + Language (L).
8. NS + CC + OC + AB + I + PT + L + Writing (W).
9. NS + CC + OC + AB + I + PT + L + W + Schooling (S).

The correspondence of each new level in the hierarchy to a faster average convergence rate has been schematized in Figure 1, in which the rates for Levels 4 through 7 are each represented by a distinct line. In general, these nine levels can be seen as but nine steps on the very long road to the type of cognitive development seen today in human cultures with educational systems.

That factors affecting convergence rate accumulate and build on one another is implicit in this hierarchical scheme. That is, new factors are added to the old without replacing the old and also depend upon the continued functioning of older factors as a context for their own operation. For present purposes, the most important property of this scheme is the critical role played by social interaction. In fact, all increases in convergence rate beyond Level 3 depend on the emergence of new forms of social interaction. Of course, that does not mean that these new forms of social interaction tell the whole story of the vastly improved convergence rates found beyond the third level. Nevertheless, that story will remain incomprehensible without an analysis of the distinct contribution of each new level of social interaction.

Before turning to an example of what such an analysis involves, it will be helpful to review what has been asserted thus far in this section. First, social facilitation of cognitive development was defined as a matter of helping a youngster close the gap between some current level of skill and the potential skill level defined by capacity limits. Then a special case of such gap-closing was discussed, the case where some other individual already possessed the expertise that would be gained by closing the gap. Finally, it was argued that the speed with which a youngster closes the gap (converges) is a function of the level of social interaction between apprentice and expert. So the main point has been that social interaction facilitates the realization of a youngster's cognitive potential. However, if we reexamine the Convergence Rate Hierarchy and think in evolutionary terms, a deeper point springs into view. It seems that, in the human lineage, newly evolved cognitive potentials have invariably been accompanied by newly evolved social-interactive modes that work to ensure full realization of the new cognitive potentials.

Let us consider Levels 4 through 7 of the hierarchy as a specific example of this point. Level 4 differs from Level 3 by the addition of a social component—the affective bond. Such a bond between the offspring and the parent ensures that the young will stay close to the parent. Maintaining this proximity with the "expert" has an immediate cognitive and adaptive payoff, since following the parent can lead the offspring to inadvertently internalize (without truly imitating) the adult's acquired patterns of spatial exploration and dietary preferences (Bullock and Neuringer, 1977). Moreover, by ensuring proximity, an affective bond also creates the minimal conditions for evolution of the capacity and skills needed for true imitation and thus the transition to Level 5 in the hierarchy. That is, without guaranteed proximity to a model, an individual's nascent imitative skill would go largely unused and therefore would not provide an adaptive advantage. But with the guarantee of proximity, nascent imitative skills would pay off quickly where rapid convergence to an expert skill level was an adaptive necessity.

We now can imagine the standard picture painted in much of social learning theory: The youngster has the cognitive capacity needed to imitate models, and his or her learning from those models is modulated by affective bonds and by reinforcement contingencies. However, the full power of imitation as a facilitator of cognitive development is not revealed until it is combined with the distinguishing element of Level 6 in the hierarchy — purposive teaching by the model (Kaye, 1982; Moerk, 1976). To understand why, a quick review of the nature of imitation as described in the literature is in order. Many psychologists continue to think of imitation as merely a faculty for automatic parroting rather than as an important developmental process. However, psychologists who have actually studied the phenomenon (Bandura, 1971; Guillaume [1926], 1971; Kaye, 1982; Piaget, 1962) discuss imitation as a process in which an observer adopts the goal of replicating some aspect of a model's activity and then spontaneously reorganizes his or her own behavior in an attempt to achieve that goal. In short, imitation is a type of goal-directed action, in which the goal happens to be that of using one's own activity to replicate some aspect of another's activity. Sometimes this goal will be trivially easy for the observer to attain (automatic), but often it will require an extended bit of problem solving — sufficient problem solving, in fact, to involve the sort of qualitative reorganization we call skill acquisition or cognitive development (Bullock, 1981).

Now let us consider two scenarios. In the first, a youngster follows her parent, observes her parent's behavior, and occasionally tries to replicate a performance she observes. But the parent merely directs an occasional act of physical nurturance toward the child. Under such conditions, imitative attempts that require extended problem solving probably would not succeed before something happened to disrupt the occasion. The second scenario adds one element to the first: The scope of the parent's nurturance has been expanded to include monitoring of, and support for, the child's imitative attempts. Such nurturance closes what we will call a *modeling circuit* between parent and child and thereby greatly increases the child's chances that his or her imitative attempts will achieve at least partial success. In most discussions of human imitation, the degree to which its success depends on purposive teaching by the model is often overlooked. Indeed, it seems that the child's imitative ability has two complementary components: one that is located in the child and one located in the teacher/model. Human imitation is thus a socially distributed or collaborative ability (Fischer and Bullock, forthcoming; Kaye, 1982).

When purposive teaching is used to close the modeling circuit, several critical precursors of the next level of social interaction—true language at Level 7—have finally been set in place. Whenever a model slows a demonstration or breaks a complex act into parts for the benefit of the observer, that model exhibits, without using language, the adjustments to the observer's comprehension level that are also a critical part of motherese. Moreover, interaction in the nonritualized domain of imitation involves a mutually recognized topic (the imitative attempt), whose content is open-ended to a degree that had never been true of social interaction built around reproduction, aggression, physical nurturance, and so forth (see Bruner, 1975). Given these precursors, both the capacity for language and particular linguistic structures could gradually evolve as yet another natural consequence of the interaction between the nurturant activity of the parent and the imitative activity of the child.

To summarize the argument thus far, upward shifts in cognitive capacity enable the development of new, more complex forms of social interaction. Shifts in the form of social interaction are now being studied throughout the period from birth to young adulthood. For example, mothers seem to alter the form and content of their speech to their children when the children undergo capacity shifts. In this section, I argued that each newly evolved level of social interaction—and each new level developed by the child—brings with it an increase in the rate at which an apprentice can converge toward expert-level performance of some skill. The highest levels of cognitive capacity, which involve language, written communication, and schooling, probably depended for their evolution on the social-interactive infrastructure represented by imitation and purposive teaching (Levels 5 and 6 of the Convergence Rate Hierarchy).

The Role of Social Interaction in the Development of the Higher Cognitive Functions

Misunderstandings abound concerning the question of whether social interaction plays a constitutive role in the development of the cognitive functions that make humans unique. To begin with, the claim that social interaction plays a constitutive role is logically distinct from the weaker claim that social interaction facilitates cognitive development. The distinction is best seen by asking what would happen if social interaction were removed from the developmental picture. Would it remain possible (disregarding time constraints due to critical periods or short life spans) for cognitive function X (for instance, symbolic thought) to develop? If so, then social interaction is only a facilitator of function X. If not—that is, if a cognitive function such as symbolic thought cannot develop without social interaction—then social interaction plays a truly constitutive role.

The Vygotskyan tradition of cognitive-developmental analysis is most closely associated with the claim that social interaction plays a constitutive role in all the higher cognitive functions (Vygotsky, [1934], 1962; Wertsch, 1979). Whereas American social learning theorists have focused on behavioral change without providing an explicit treatment of levels of behavioral organization, Russian social learning theorists have looked closely at several levels of organization from a social perspective (Wertsch, 1981). According to Vygotsky and his followers, all higher cognitive functions have a similar developmental history. First, they are formed on what Vygotsky calls the *interpsychological plane* — that is, worked out by two cooperating individuals, both of whom are needed to establish and perform the function. Only then, after being socially constituted, can the new function be internalized by either person and performed on the *intrapsychological plane*. Once this internalization has occurred, the social origin of the function is usually forgotten.

Vygotsky and his followers claim that symbolic, or language-based, thinking is a classic example of a socially constituted function. Of course, many other theorists consider symbolic thinking to be an asocial activity, and in one sense it is: An individual can think symbolically without immediate accommodation to others. But, if Vygotsky is right, such activity is essentially social in a deeper sense. The form of symbolic-thinking activity reflects a long history of prior accommodation to others, and the activity itself would never have come to exist without social interaction. Regarding the form of the activity, Vygotskyans note that advanced thinking — the sort that produces conceptual innovations in children and adults alike — actually has the character of an internal dialogue. The thinker poses questions, then provides provisional answers, questions their adequacy, tries reformulations, and so on. Moreover, the arguments of Vygotsky and others (Bickhard, 1980; Kaye, 1982; Wittgenstein, 1953) are not based solely on the dialogical format of symbolic thought. Such thought is also supported and constrained by socially evolved category systems. For example, when we think of "doe," we can hardly help thinking of "mammal" and then perhaps of other parts of the system of biological taxonomy and its modern evolutionary justification. This train of thought would be unavailable to us if we could not use socially defined symbols.

Finally, the most important justification for the Vygotsky argument is that the use of symbols itself depends on one's ability to participate in symbolization, which is an inherently social process. Many fail to understand that the symbolic function is socially constituted because they misconstrue what is meant by symbolization. Symbolization is not the isolated thinker's act of representing a symbol to him- or herself. In fact, although symbolization is based on the capacity for internal representation, it should not be classified as a type of internal representation at all. Instead it is a social act of agreeing with another person to assign a particular meaning to a packet of sounds, a configuration of the hand, or a bunch of squiggles on a piece of paper. It is a matter, then, of establishing a social convention — something that logically requires a minimum of two agents. Every symbol is a residue of such an act of social agreement. To the extent that the higher psychological functions depend on the use of symbols, such functions are thus validly seen as socially constituted. The level of social interaction required for spontaneous symbolization is unique to human beings. Thus, it is quite possible that all the unique accomplishments of human beings stem from the special type of thinking made possible by social acts of symbolization, the shared symbol systems produced by such acts, and the very rapid cognitive convergence made possible by widespread sharing of such symbol systems.

Conclusion

In this chapter, motherese, the proposed Convergence Rate Hierarchy, and symbolization have been used as vehicles to emphasize the complementary roles of cognitive growth and social interaction in human development. The study of this complementarity leads, in turn, to an emphasis on two general principles, some of whose implications extend beyond the scope of this chapter. First, a type of nurture can be a product of nature. Besides summarizing the main point of the Convergence Rate Hierarchy, this principle implies a dissolution of the classical nature-nurture dispute. After all, the social-interactive nurture that validly looms so large in many accounts of normative child development is itself a many-layered, evolving phenomenon. Second, cognitive potential co-evolves with mechanisms for its realization. This principle restores some balance to views of human cognition that focus exclusively on large cognitive capacity or internal representational abilities. Of equal importance are the social-interactive and other guarantees that full use will be made of such capabilities.

References

Bandura, A. "Analysis of Modeling Processes." In A. Bandura (Ed.), *Psychological Modeling: Conflicting Theories.* Chicago, Ill.: Aldine, 1971.

Bandura, A. *Social Learning Theory.* Englewood Cliffs, N.J.: Prentice-Hall, 1977.

Baumrind, D. "Child Care Practices Anteceding Three Patterns of Preschool Behavior." *Genetic Psychology Monographs,* 1967, *75*, 43–88.

Bickhard, M. H. *Cognition, Convention, and Communication.* New York: Praeger, 1980.

Bruner, J. S. "From Communication to Language—A Psychological Perspective." *Cognition,* 1975, *3*, 255–287.

Bullock, D. "On the Current and Potential Scope of Generative Theories of Cognitive Development." In K. W. Fischer (Ed.), *Cognitive Development.* New Directions for Child Development, no. 12. San Francisco: Jossey-Bass, 1981.

Bullock, D., and Neuringer, A. J. "Social Learning by Following: An Analysis." *Journal of the Experimental Analysis of Behavior,* 1977, *27*, 127–135.

Butterworth, G., and Light, P. *Social Cognition.* Chicago: University of Chicago Press, 1982.

Cross, T. G. "Mothers' Speech Adjustments: The Contribution of Selected Child Listener Variables." In C. E. Snow and C. A. Ferguson (Eds.), *Talking to Children:*

Language Input and Acquisition. Cambridge, England: Cambridge University Press, 1977.

Dennett, D. C. "Why the Law of Effect Will Not Go Away." *Journal for the Theory of Social Behavior,* 1975, *5,* 169–187.

Fischer, K. W. "A Theory of Cognitive Development: The Control and Construction of Hierarchies of Skills." *Psychological Review,* 1980, *87,* 477–531.

Fischer, K. W., and Bullock, D. "Patterns of Data: Sequence, Synchrony, and Constraint in Cognitive Development." In K. W. Fischer (Ed.), *Cognitive Development.* New Directions for Child Development, no. 12. San Francisco: Jossey-Bass, 1981.

Fischer, K. W., and Bullock, D. "Cognitive Development in School-Aged Children: Conclusions and New Directions." In W. A. Collins (Ed.), *Basic Research on School-Age Children.* Washington, D.C.: National Academy Press, forthcoming.

Fischer, K. W., Pipp, S. L., and Bullock, D. "Detecting Developmental Discontinuities: Method and Measurement." In R. Harmon and R. N. Emde (Eds.), *Continuities and Discontinuities in Development.* New York: Plenum, forthcoming.

Fischer, K. W., and Watson, M. W. "Explaining the Oedipus Conflict." In K. W. Fischer (Ed.), *Cognitive Development.* New Directions for Child Development, no. 12. San Francisco: Jossey-Bass, 1981.

Flavell, J. H. "On Cognitive Development." *Child Development,* 1982, *53,* 1–10.

Guillaume, P. *Imitation in Children.* Chicago: University of Chicago Press, 1971. (Original French edition 1926.)

Kaye, K. *The Mental and Social Life of Babies.* Chicago: University of Chicago Press, 1982.

Kelley, H. H., and Thibaut, J. W. *Interpersonal Relations: A Theory of Interdependence.* New York: Wiley, 1978.

Maccoby, E. E. *Social Development.* New York: Harcourt Brace Jovanovich, 1980.

Moerk, E. "Processes of Language Teaching and Training in the Interactions of Mother–Child Dyads." *Child Development,* 1976, *47,* 1064–1078.

Olson, D. R. *The Social Foundations of Language and Thought.* New York: Norton, 1980.

Piaget, J. *Play, Dreams, and Imitation in Children.* New York: Norton, 1962.

Rogoff, B., Sellers, M. J., Pirotta, S., Fox, N., and White, S. H. "Age of Assignment of Roles and Responsibilities to Children." *Human Development,* 1975, *18,* 353–369.

Vygotsky, L. S. *Thought and Language.* Cambridge: MIT Press, 1962. (Original Russian edition 1934.)

Wertsch, J. V. "From Social Interaction to Higher Psychological Processes." *Human Development,* 1979, *22,* 1–22.

Wertsch, J. V. *The Concept of Activity in Soviet Psychology.* New York: Sharpe, 1981.

Wittgenstein, L. *Philosophical Investigations.* New York: Macmillan, 1953.

Youniss, J. *Parents and Peers in Social Development: A Sullivan-Piaget Perspective.* Chicago: University of Chicago Press, 1982.

Daniel Bullock is assistant professor of psychology at the University of Denver. His research deals with the role of the social environment in cognitive and language development and the theory of goal selection in development.

Index

A

Abstract mappings level, and discontinuities, 83, 89
Abstract systems level, and discontinuities, 83, 89
Active thought: analysis of dawn of, 37–50; background on, 37–39; implications of findings on, 46–48; and object use, 43–45; and processing nonsocial stimuli, 39–41; and social behavior, 45–46; and vocalization and pointing to social stimuli, 41–43
Adams, A., 97n
Adelson, J., 14, 18, 83, 93
Adolescence: assessment problems in, 90–91; developmental discontinuity in, 88–89
Adulthood, developmental discontinuities in, 89–90
Appelbaum, M. I., 79
Arlin, P. K., 89, 93
Attention, study of, 39–40

B

Ball, R. S., 48, 49, 68, 79
Bandura, A., 101, 104, 107
Basseches, M., 85, 90, 93
Bates, E., 52, 55, 62
Bayley, N., 31, 34, 42, 48, 74, 75, 78
Bayley Scales of Infant Development, 13, 31, 33, 47, 70
Behavior: developments in, and physical growth, 31, 33; social, and active thought, 45–46
Belsky, J., 44, 48
Berkeley Growth Study, and transitions in mental development, 69–74
Bertenthal, B., 53, 62
Bever, T. G., 22, 34
Bickhard, M. H., 106, 107
Biggs, J. B., 6, 10, 14, 15, 16, 83, 85, 86n, 87, 88, 93
Bloom, B. S., 66–67, 78
Bowerman, M., 55, 62
Brain development, levels in, 16–17

Briars, D. J., 19
Broughton, J. M., 5, 18, 85, 86, 90, 93
Bruner, J. S., 42, 48, 87, 93, 105, 107
Bruskin, C., 55, 63
Bullock, D., 1, 2, 3, 5, 6, 10, 11, 12, 15, 16, 18, 19, 38, 49, 82, 88, 91, 94, 97–108
Butterworth, G., 97, 107

C

Cameron, N., 22, 35
Canfield, R., 5n
Carnegie Corporation of New York, 1n, 5n, 37n, 81n
Case, R., 7, 10, 14, 15, 18, 85, 86, 87, 88, 94
Change: as continuous or discontinuous, 66; importance of, 65–66
Child development: and active thought, 37–50; and childhood and adolescent discontinuities, 81–95; cognitive development and social interaction in, 97–108; conclusions on, 2–3; and episodic growth, 21–36; levels as discontinuities in, 5–20; and representational skills, 51–64; and transitions in mental development, 65–79
Children: developmental discontinuities among, 85–87; developmental levels of retarded or handicapped, 13; and environment in collaboration, 15–17; at 1 to 2 months, 74; at 2 to 4 months, 11–13, 23, 34, 55, 71–73, 74; at 7 to 8 months, 12, 13, 23, 34, 55, 67–69, 72–73, 74; at 11 to 13 months, 12, 13, 23, 37–50, 55, 57, 62, 67–69, 72–73, 74; at 18 to 24 months, 12, 13, 23, 51–64, 67–69, 72–73, 74; at 4 to 5 years, 12, 14, 85, 86, 87, 89, 93; at 6 to 8 years, 12, 14, 84, 85, 86, 87, 89, 93; at 10 to 12 years, 12, 14, 83–84, 85, 86, 87–88, 89, 93; at 14 to 16 years, 12, 15, 83, 85, 86, 88–89, 93; at 17 to 21 years, 84, 86, 89; at 24 to 26 years, 86, 89
Chomsky, N., 101